Newborn

Newborn

HAROLD M. FRELIGH

A Basic Handbook on Salvation
for Personal or Group Study

Newborn
by Harold M. Freligh
Originally published under the title,
The Eight Pillars of Salvation

Reprinted in 1994
by ICI University Press
6300 North Belt Line Road
Irving, Texas 75063 USA
by permission of Bethany Fellowship, Inc.
11/94 1M EP

Printed in Colombia

DEDICATION

To the many students
scattered over the world,
whose classroom comradeship
has enriched my life.

FOREWORD

The Scripture tells us that the worlds were framed by the Word of God and that things seen came out of things unseen. The world is neither self-existent nor self-perpetuating; it is the effect of a previous Cause and is kept in being by the creative Word, which continues to speak and to be spoken throughout the whole creation. "In the beginning was the Word, and the Word was with God, and the Word was God. . . . All things were made by him; and without him was not any thing made that was made."

The Scriptures also teach that the Creator set a crown upon His work by making man in His own image and likeness. Man is essentially spiritual. We must think of him not as having a soul but as *being* a soul. He must be understood not as a physical body having a spirit, but as a spirit having a body.

This being so, no science is true science that deals with God's handiwork while ignoring God; and no philosophy is sound philosophy that fails to take into account man's spiritual origin. Man's explanation lies not in man but in God. For this reason all man's problems are at bottom theological and all their solutions spiritual.

It follows that the most important study for any man is not science nor philosophy but theology. In true theology lies the answer to every question concerning man's origin, man's moral and social responsibilities and man's destiny. Neither philosophy nor science can answer man's *basic* questions, whereas these are precisely the questions Christian theology does answer accurately and finally.

The world does not know it, and I am afraid that the Church herself does not always remember it, but the most important book is always the one that sets forth most clearly the truths of Christian theology. For sheer usefulness to the human race no book dealing with the world of politics or science, or any other subject bounded by time and space, is remotely to be compared with the book that deals with Christian theology. Man was made for eternity and can never be finally satisfied with anything temporal.

The failure of contemporary Christianity to understand the vital importance of theology has greatly weakened the churches and given us a scrubby and degenerate type of Christian that can scarcely be distinguished from the sons of this world. A flabby humanism of the modern church, touched lightly with pale and bloodless Christianity, is not producing spiritual giants these days. The tall sons of God must be nourished on strong meat, and little is being offered them but religious milk from which most of the cream has been taken.

The appearance of a good, readable book dealing with basic Christianity is an event, and should be welcomed with enthusiasm. *Newborn* is such a book. It is frankly a book on Christian doctrine, especially the doctrine of salvation as it affects the individual Christian. It does not strain after effects nor try to be "original," but stays close to the Word of God in mood, in language and in purpose. The urgency of the true Christian teacher may be felt throughout it.

The author uses both the negative and positive method to make his ideas clear to the reader, often employing both in the same sentence. By the process of eliminating erroneous notions concerning the truth, he makes the truth itself stand out sharp and clear when he at last enunciates it. He draws skillful contrasts between ideas that resemble each other but are not identical, and thus clears up much of the confusion that has gathered around them.

Some brief examples of this method may be given here. In his chapter on repentance he says, "Repentance is not the same as remorse. Remorse is a dead-end street; repentance is a highway. Remorse looks at our sins only; repentance looks beyond our sins to Calvary. Remorse turns us back on ourselves; repentance turns us to God." And what could be plainer or neater than these definitions: "Regeneration is a change of our nature. Justification is a change of our standing before God. Adoption is a change of our rank and position."

This is primarily a textbook, but it is not so technical as to limit it to the classroom. It would make an excellent book for the pastor to use in his weekly instruction classes for young Christians. And if some adventurous Sunday school teacher were to depart from the prescribed lesson and for one quarter follow this book as a guide for the indoctrination of his pupils, who can predict what benefits might result? The last chapter shows how the book may be used in this way.

I trust that *Newborn* will find a great many readers. It will bear everlasting fruit in the lives of those who are willing to give it time and attention.

A. W. Tozer

Toronto, Ontario
Canada

PREFACE

Salvation represents all that was purchased at Calvary. It covers every phase of our need, and reaches from eternity to eternity. It includes forgiveness of sins of the past, deliverance from sin's power in the present, and preservation against sin's invasions in the future (Jude 24, 25).

Salvation is both a future prospect and a present enjoyment (Titus 2:11–13). But there are many Christians who know nothing, or little, concerning salvation as a present enjoyment. They think of it only as a means of getting to heaven. Unless heaven begins in the heart down here, no soul is prepared to enter its glory up there.

Our spiritual growth should begin as soon as we know the Saviour and His salvation. A stunted Christian is no credit to Christ and His power to save. He lacks spiritual nourishment, and consequently spiritual development.

Two hindrances to spiritual development are ignorance and apathy. The first can be cured by reading the Word and learning the wealth of our salvation. The second is cured by the Holy Spirit's work in the heart that becomes obedient to Him and receives the hunger and thirst for righteousness that characterizes a healthy spiritual appetite.

The purpose of this book is to bring to the child of God a better understanding of his salvation, and thus further his spiritual progress. It is a sketchy study of topics that are theologically known as soteriology, which simply means the doctrine of salvation. The studies have grown out of many years of instruction to young people who are now scattered over the world, and of whom I fondly think as my children.

It is my hope that these simple studies will bring to an enlarged circle a fuller understanding of salvation, together with a consequent growth in grace and the knowledge of our Lord and Saviour, Jesus Christ.

H.M.F.

La Crescenta, California
April 1962

TABLE OF CONTENTS

INTRODUCTION

Salvation may be defined as the full doctrine of redemption, accomplished by Christ through His death and resurrection. Our salvation is founded on the Rock, Christ Jesus. But, like the pillars of a beautiful temple supported by a foundation, there are eight phases of God's purpose and privilege for each Christian. Some of them every Christian has learned to appreciate and appropriate. Others of them many Christians have not examined, or else have examined so little that they know neither what they are nor how to apply them gratefully to their own lives.

Many persons have an earthly inheritance but do not know it. The courts are still searching for heirs who have not claimed sums of money left them. Other persons have an inheritance that they are not putting to use. In spite of their hoarded gold they live like paupers. Many Christians are experiencing the same thing spiritually. Some of them do not know what they possess in Christ. This is because they have not studied carefully the will and testament left them by the Saviour. Others know more than they appropriate. Indifference can be a greater thief than ignorance. When the enlightened intellect is spurred by a will that is fired with desire for God's complete purpose, then we reach out and receive what is ours. Why not enjoy our inheritance?

The eight pillars of salvation are *repentance, faith, conversion, regeneration, justification, adoption, sanctification,* and *prayer*. They do not necessarily represent a chronological order. Many of them run concurrently. Taken all together, they form what is known theologically as *soteriology*, which simply means the doctrine of salvation. Salvation is not used here in the limited sense of the initial act of receiving Christ, by which act one becomes a son of God (John 1.12). It is used in the broad sense, including (1) forgiveness of sins and the accompanying consciousness of a cleansed conscience; (2) victory over the sinful nature, which causes defeat in one's life; (3) the various phases and results of Christ's redemptive work both *for* us objectively and *in* us subjectively; (4) and our final deliverance when our bodies are changed, resurrected, and glorified at the return of our Lord Jesus Christ.

A study of these eight topics ushers us further into our temple of worship, with a fuller understanding of the wonder of being a Christian. Come, let us enter in.

Newborn

CHAPTER ONE

REPENTANCE

Definition of Repentance

Repentance is that act whereby one recognizes and turns from his sin, confessing it to God. Its subsequent correlative is faith in Christ. The two together—repentance and faith—constitute conversion. To this may be added God's work of forgiveness.

"Repentance toward God and faith toward our Lord Jesus Christ" (Acts 20:21) necessarily go together. Repentance toward God is encouraged by the knowledge that God is propitious toward the sinner, not in overlooking his sin but in sending His Son to die in the sinner's place. Faith toward Christ is encouraged by an understanding of the purpose and meaning of His death. It is the preaching of the cross, then, that induces both repentance and faith.

To preach repentance without including the message of the cross is like giving a car empty of gas a push downhill where it will soon stop. To include the cross in the preaching of repentance is like putting gas in the car, and then bidding the driver step on it so as to bring him up to Mt. Calvary and Christ Jesus.

The incentive for turning from sin is recognition of its offence against God. The incentive for turning to Christ is a realization of His work in atoning for our sins.

Repentance is not the same as *remorse*. Repentance is not at the same time a professed sorrow for sin and a willing continuation in sin. It is possible to feel sorry for our sins and yet have no desire to quit sinning. Many a sinner is not ready to repent because he is not ready to give up his sins. John is caught cheating in his examination. He is penalized by receiving an F. He is sorry he has been caught, but the times he has not been caught bother him not a whit. He is remorseful but not repentant, and is just as ready to cheat again if he can get by with it. Ed has cheated without being caught, but his conscience bothers him. Finally he goes to his professor, confesses the whole thing, and offers to take any penalty imposed upon him. He is repentant and ready to quit the cheating business. Heaven is full of repentant onetime sinners; hell is full of remorseful ones.

The rich man in Hades cried out for mercy, and wanted someone to warn his brothers lest they come to the same place of torment (Luke 16:24–28). He was full of remorse, but he was too late to repent. Those who do not repent now will one day weep, and wail, and gnash their teeth (Matt. 13:42, 50; Luke 13:38)— in remorse but not in repentance. They will be willing for the rocks and mountains to fall and cover them (Rev. 6:15–17) because they were never willing to turn from their sin and repent.

Remorse is a dead-end street; repentance is a highway.

Remorse looks at our sins only; repentance looks beyond our sins to Calvary.

Remorse turns us back on ourselves; repentance turns us to God.

Remorse makes us hate ourselves, though we may be loving our sins at the same time; repentance makes us hate our sins and love our Saviour in one act.

Remorse is the sorrow of the world which "worketh death"; repentance is "godly sorrow" which leads to salvation (II Cor. 7:10).

Repentance is not making *resolutions*, or turning over a new leaf. New Year's resolutions hardly outlast January 1. The new leaf soon becomes stained. The reason that a resolution to change one's course is not repentance is that repentance involves an attitude toward God, while a resolution involves an attitude toward one's failure and himself. No one truly repents unless and until he sees something of the heinousness of his sin in God's sight.

Repentance is not the same as doing *penance*. Repentance is united to faith in Christ, while doing penance is tinged with the idea of gaining merit before God. Nothing can be added to Christ's work as far as atoning for our sins is concerned. Moreover, one might do penance without breaking from his sin, and might think that he can continue in sin as long as he continues doing acts of penance.

The word *repentance* literally means "a change of mind." This indicates that repentance is a mental attitude toward sin; the will is involved, as well as the intellect and the emotions.

According to Spurgeon *legal repentance* is a fear of damnation; *evangelical repentance* is a fear of sinning. *Legal repentance* makes us fear the wrath of God; *evangelical repentance* makes us fear the cause of that wrath, which is sin. To advance from the fear of God's wrath to the fear of causing that wrath is to make progress in repentance.

Repentance is like a triangle—it has three sides. And, just as it takes all three sides to make a triangle, so all three aspects constitute repentance.

(1) The *intellectual aspect*. There must be a recognition of our condition and of what sin is. By sin is meant any act, disposition, or state that is contrary to God and His will. We can find what God's will is in His Word, the Scriptures. We should know God's "Thou shalts" as well as His "Thou shalt nots." Before anyone repents, he must recognize that he personally has sinned. Particularly he must see that sin, his sin, is an outrage against God. This is more than a recognition of sin's consequences. An outright and full confession of sin involves a realization that sin offends a holy God.

In David's great penitential prayer, he confessed, "Against thee, thee only, have I sinned, and done this evil in thy sight" (Psa. 51:4). David had committed two high crimes against society. One was adultery, and the other was murder. Yet, in confessing his sin, he acknowledged that it had been against God. This is what made his sorrow penetrating and his repentance thorough.

Hear the confession of the prodigal son: "Father, I have sinned against heaven, and in thy sight" (Luke 15:21). Could it be that his dissolute life had affected heaven? When he saw that, he was humbled to dust and ready to return to the father with no passport except his repentance.

Even those who have not committed adultery or murder or lived a riotous life need to repent, the same as David and the prodigal. Here is Saul, a self-righteous Pharisee, who lived a morally upright life, "touching the righteousness which is in the law, blameless" (Phil. 3:6). But one day at high noon on the hot road to Damascus he heard a voice: "Saul, Saul, why persecutest thou me?" (Acts 9:4). The question "why?" appealed to his intellect, his reason. And the full question "Why... *Me?*" enlightened his soul. He was brought face to face not only with his Saviour, but also with his sin. He had been persecuting Christ himself. His sin had been against God. His repentance was immediate and profound. It changed the whole course of his life.

A repentant sinner faces his sin and God at the same time. He makes no attempt to conceal it or excuse it, but he openly declares it *before God*: "I will declare mine iniquity" (Psa. 38:18a). The intellect acquiesces to what God has already stated in His Word—"All have sinned" (Rom. 3:23).

(2) The *emotional aspect*. The sense of one's sinfulness produces sorrow: "I will be sorry for my sin" (Psa. 38:18b). David mourned over his sin and prayed, "Make me to hear joy and gladness; that the bones which thou hast broken may rejoice" (Psa. 51:8). The prodigal son "came to himself," and felt regret over his wretched condition when he compared it with the hired servants in his father's house who had "bread enough and to spare." Paul was three days without food or drink (Acts 9:9) while this "chief of sinners" fed on the regret of his past career and learned the taste of God's forgiveness. It was like manna from heaven.

How many tears must one shed in order to repent? The amount of weeping does not matter because the emotions vary according to temperament. Some persons weep easily, and others rarely display any tears. Some grieve deeply without showing their sorrow, and others carry their feelings in an open basket. There is nothing wrong about the emotions; they are an important element of personality. It is the violation of them that is wrong. They must not be allowed to blow off in mere steam, but must be channeled and made to drive the piston. Unless the emotions are harnessed to the will, they become harmful.

When one repents, there will be at least some measure of sorrow because of one's sin, but our feelings must be put into action. David cried to God for forgiveness and cleansing, and asked Him to build again the walls that had been morally broken down by his failure (Psa. 51:18). The prodigal son did more than feel sorry concerning his condition; he did something about it. He arose and went to his father. When Ananias visited Saul, he at once obeyed and was baptized, and became a zealous witness for Christ (Acts 9:17–20). This leads us to the third aspect of repentance.

(3) The *volitional aspect.* This has to do with the will. The will is the base of the triangle, on which the whole rests, and is the most important feature of repentance. Not only must we recognize our sins and feel sorry because of them, but we must also confess and forsake them. If we have gone no further than the intellectual and emotional stages of repentance, we have not gone far enough. In order to be forgiven our sins, we must forsake them: "Let the wicked forsake his way . . . , and let him return unto the LORD . . . , for he will abundantly pardon" (Isa. 55:7). A man who comes up to repentance faces a fork in the road, and the path he chooses determines his destiny: "He that covereth his sins shall not prosper; but whoso confesseth and forsaketh them shall have mercy" (Prov. 28:13). Which shall it be, further failure or divine mercy?

Repentance and Restitution

When one makes restitution—pays back what he has wrongfully taken—that is a good evidence that his repentance is genuine. It has struck root so deeply that this fruit of making amends is produced. John the Baptist spoke about "fruits worthy of repentance" (Luke 3:8). Zacchaeus was ready to restore fourfold what he had extorted by false accusation (Luke 19:8). Restitution gives weight to the testimony of a man who professes to have repented and to have turned to Christ. Restitution does not save, for we are saved by grace; but restitution declares to God and to man that we have forsaken the old paths. It is the confirmation of our decision to turn from sin to Christ. It is a practical accompaniment to our verbal testimony before men concerning the new Master we are following. It is not meritorious as a means of salvation, but it is a worthy indication of it.

When to Preach and Practice Repentance

Repentance is part of the message for this church age. On the day of Pentecost, the birthday of the Church, Peter called upon his audience to repent: "Repent, and be baptized every one of you in the name of Jesus Christ for the remission of your sins" (Acts 2:38).

Paul preached repentance to the assembly on Mars' Hill in Athens: "God ... commandeth all men everywhere to repent" (Acts 17:30). He also preached it in Ephesus, and later reminded the elders there that among them he had preached "repentance toward God" (Acts 20:21).

Jesus included repentance as part of the message of the great commission to the whole world: "And that repentance and remission of sins should be preached in his name among all nations" (Luke 24:47).

We are quite in order when we follow the example set by the apostles and the command given by our

Lord. As long as there is need for salvation from sin, there is need for repentance because of it. It has always been so since the day of man's fall, and will always be so until the present era of grace and opportunity to repent comes to a close.

Who Should Repent

Everyone is called upon to repent. This includes those who are not yet Christians because they have not placed personal faith in Christ. They are termed unbelievers because they have not personally believed in Christ, though they may have believed *about* Him. They are called upon to repent. God "commandeth all men everywhere to repent" (Acts 17:30). Since sin is universal, the call to repentance is universal.

Believers, those who are Christians because of personal faith in Christ, are also called to repentance. The Ephesian church was commanded to repent because she had left her first love (Rev. 2:5). Jesus also commanded the lukewarm Laodicean church to repent: "As many as I love, I rebuke and chasten: be zealous therefore, and repent" (Rev. 3:19).

Repentance is the way back to God wherever there has been failure and sin. The promise of God's forgiveness if we confess our sins (I John 1:9) is primarily for Christians, though it is applicable to anyone who is ready to repent.

Why Men Should Repent

We should repent because we have sinned. This includes everyone. A person is just as guilty for failing to do right as for doing wrong. The watchman who fails to put down the gates, and allows the oncoming train to hit and kill five persons in the auto on the railroad tracks is as guilty of murder as the hit-and-run driver who leaves his victim dead in the wake of his recklessness. The former is a sin of omission; the latter, of commission. "Therefore to him that knoweth to do good, and doeth it not, to him it is sin" (James 4:17). This is the sin of omission. "Sin is the transgression of the law" (I John 3:4). This is the sin of commission. Either one is an evidence of unrighteousness, and "all unrighteousness is sin" (I John 5:17).

According to the legal definition, "A crime is an act or an omission forbidden by law." Both by the statements of man's law, and by the declaration of God's Word, we are guilty. The law demands payment of the penalty, but God offers pardon for those who repent and accept His forgiveness through the blood of Jesus Christ. One is foolish indeed who refuses to humble himself in repentance and accept God's grace.

How Repentance is Produced

Repentance is a gift from God: "If God peradventure will give them repentance to the acknowledging of the truth" (II Tim. 2:25). It is the "goodness of God" that leads to repentance (Rom. 2:4).

The preaching of the Word of God also brings repentance. Nineveh repented through Jonah's preaching. Because of that preaching the king decreed, "Let man and beast be covered with sackcloth, and cry mightily unto God; yea, let them turn every one from his evil way, and from the violence that is in their hands" (Jonah 3:8). The outcome was that the whole city was spared.

Even opposers may be led to repentance through instruction in the Word: "In meekness instructing those that oppose themselves; if God peradventure will give them repentance to the acknowledging of the truth" (II Tim. 2:25).

The preaching of the cross produces repentance. God's love as revealed at Calvary breaks the stony heart. Such a message appeals to the one who knows he is a sinner and is morally sick. His ear is open to the call of repentance. "For I am not come to call the righteous, but sinners to repentance" (Matt. 9:13; Mark 2:17; Luke 5:32). The inhabitants of Jerusalem will repent when at Christ's return they look upon Him "whom they have pierced" (Zech. 12:10). To see the pierced One is to be pierced by repentance.

A vision of God also produces repentance. Job's self-righteousness wilted to death before God's white righteousness: "I have heard of thee by the hearing of the ear: but now mine eye seeth thee. Wherefore I abhor myself, and repent in dust and ashes" (Job 42:5, 6).

The Outcome of Repentance

Repentance produces joy in the presence of the angels. It affects not only one's own life but also heaven. "There is joy in the presence of the angels of God over one sinner that repenteth" (Luke 15:10). When a penitent turns from his sin to Christ, he pulls the rope that sets the joybells in the sky ringing.

Repentance is the forerunner of faith. It is because we see God's mercy in giving His Son to die for us that we are encouraged to repent and confess our sins to Him.

Repentance leads to forgiveness. When we confess our sins and turn to God through the merits of Jesus Christ, He forgives our sins (I John 1:9).

Repentance, faith, and forgiveness are all links in the chain of conversion. Each one is separate, yet each one is for the purpose of being joined to the others. No link can be omitted, for each has its own value in this beautiful work of conversion.

CHAPTER TWO

FAITH

Definition of Faith

Faith is that voluntary act and attitude of the individual whereby he places the weight of his need upon and governs his actions by a trusted object. In the Scriptural realm the trusted object is God, and the voluntary act is induced by hearing believingly His Word.

"Now faith is the substance of things hoped for, the evidence of things not seen" (Heb. 11:1). This Scriptural definition tells how faith works. It is "the giving substance to things hoped for, a conviction of things not seen" (A.R.V. m.)—that is, faith operates in a realm other than sight or outward, tangible evidence. The writer to the Hebrews goes on to prove and explain his point by saying that "the worlds were framed by the word of God, so that things which are seen were not made of things which do appear" (vs. 3).

Characteristics of Faith

Faith has no intruders between itself and God. It does not believe *about* Christ, but believes Christ himself. It is not a leap into the dark; it is supported by God's eternal Word.

Faith is not the same as hope, though it is related to it.

Hope is our aspiration; faith, our foundation.

Without hope the Christian's life would be drab; without faith it would collapse.

Hope transports us to the future and has patience as its handmaid: "But if we hope for that we see not, then do we with patience wait for it" (Rom. 8:25).

Faith transports the future to us and generates patience by being tested: "Knowing this, that the trying of your faith worketh patience" (James 1:3).

Hope makes God's promises a bright expectation. Many persons think they are trusting God's promise when they are simply hoping that it will come to pass.

Faith makes the promises so real that we can embrace them or greet them "from afar" (Heb. 11:13, A.R.V.).

"Hope maketh not ashamed" (Rom. 5:5).
Faith gives us access "into this grace wherein we stand" (Rom. 5:2).

Faith is not an emotion that passes *over* us but a conviction that operates *through* us. The former (emotion) is the needle on the face of a record, producing sounds; the latter (conviction) is the performer himself pouring forth his heart. The former (emotion) is the brook turning the water wheel; the latter (conviction) is the miller operating all the affairs of his plant. The understanding, the emotions, and the will are all cooperative and combined in the exercise of faith. Andrew Murray says, "To believe truly is to will firmly."

The use of the will in the exercise of faith is manifested by obedience. Obedience and faith, therefore, are doctrinally synonymous. "He that believeth on the Son hath eternal life; but he that *obeyeth not* the Son [A.R.V.] shall not see life" (John 3:36). It is impossible to believe God without obeying Him. This is not the obedience of a child who is forced to do what he does not want to, but it is the cooperation of a child who seeks to please his parents by fulfilling their desires.

Conversely, unbelief is disobedience. The sad example of this is the failure of God's people to enter Canaan: "And to whom sware he that they should not enter into his rest, but to them that were *disobedient?* And we see that they were not able to enter in because of *unbelief*" (Heb. 3:18, 19, A.R.V.). They "failed to enter in because of *disobedience*" (Heb. 6:11, A.R.V.). We cannot disobey God and have faith in Him at the same time. To be in the realm of faith we must keep His commandments: "And whatsoever we ask, we receive of him, because we keep his commandments, and do those things that are pleasing in his sight" (I John 3:22).

Faith does not look within, or around, but above— "Looking unto Jesus the author and finisher of our faith" (Heb. 12:2). It does not feel its own pulse or question its own condition. Like a healthy body whose organs function without conscious effort, so faith works by union with God, who is life. It is a fruit of the Spirit (Gal. 5:22).

If our faith is weak, it is because our vision of Jesus Christ, the Object of our faith, is blurred. When we look at the raging waves around us, we, like Peter, commence to sink. Faith does not feed on doubts but on the promises of God. It is by keeping our eyes on Jesus that we reach our goal.

If there is trembling, it is we who are doing the shaking and not the Rock beneath us. To be conscious of our own weakness is to waver; to be conscious of our strong Foundation is to stand firm. Abraham did not count on his own dead body nor the deadness of Sarah's womb; he counted on God's promise: "Yet, looking unto the promise of God, he wavered not through unbelief, but waxed strong through faith, giving glory to God, and being fully assured that what he had promised, he was able also to perform" (Rom. 4:20, 21, A.R.V.).

Faith operates according to certain principles that are as workable as any other of God's laws, natural or spiritual. "Faith in God so unites us to God that it passes beyond the privilege of asking to the power of commanding."—A. T. Pierson.

Faith is not a static attainment but a living principle. It is not an emblem that we wear on our chest, but a seed planted in the heart. It germinates and grows. Jesus compared it to a grain of mustard seed.

Degrees of Faith

Since faith is a living principle, it has stages. Paul desired to perfect that which was *lacking* in the faith of the Thessalonians (I Thess. 3:10). Their faith had started to grow, but needed maturing. In his second epistle Paul commends them for the *growth* of their faith—"We are bound to thank God always for you, brethren. . . , because that your faith groweth exceedingly" (II Thess. 1:3). Paul also expected the Corinthians to grow in faith: "Having hope, when your faith is increased, that we shall be enlarged by you" (II Cor. 10:15). God expects this same growth of each of His children.

Little faith is not God's standard for His people. This does not contradict the little faith that is only the size of a mustard seed. The little faith spoken of under the caption in this paragraph is the kind that is so slight as to be of little help. It is a wind-shaken reed that gives meager support, or none at all. The mustard-seed faith, though small in quantity, is mighty in quality. Little faith will not protect us from *anxiety* over what we shall eat and how we shall be clothed (Matt. 6:30, 31). Little faith is not strong enough to meet the attacks of *fear*. The disciples became fearful in the storm on Galilee because of their little faith, and received a mild reproof from Jesus: "Why are ye fearful, O ye of little faith?" (Matt. 8:26). Little faith and *doubt* are often bedfellows. When Peter saw the waves instead of Jesus, fear entered, and doubt came along: "O thou of little faith, wherefore didst thou doubt?" (Matt. 14:30, 31). Little faith is not able to combat our *reasonings*. The disciples forgot how Jesus had twice fed the multitudes, and commenced to reason among themselves what they should do because they had forgotten to take bread: "O ye of little faith, why reason ye among yourselves, because ye have brought no bread?" (Matt. 16:8). God expects us to advance from this stage of faith to a higher one.

Great faith is commended by Jesus. It is unbelief, not faith, that amazed Jesus. He never marveled at any miracle He performed, but He marveled at the unbelief He found in His home country (Mark 6:6). It is significant that twice Jesus commended great faith, and it is still more significant that each time He found it in foreigners. He commended the great faith He found in the centurion who believed Jesus could heal his servant without even coming to his house: "Verily I say unto you, I have not found so great faith, no, not in Israel" (Matt. 8:10). Again He commended the Syrophoenician woman who persisted in asking for her daughter's healing: "O woman, great is thy faith: be it unto thee even as thou wilt" (Matt. 15:28).

Strong faith is what enabled Abraham to believe for the birth of Isaac when everything in the natural was against it (Rom. 4:20).

Fulness of faith gives us confidence in drawing near to God. It is like boldly presenting a check to the bank teller because we know the man who wrote it and we know his bank account. "Let us draw near with a true heart in fulness of faith" (Heb. 10:22, A.R.V.).

Tested faith produces patience, or stedfastness. The tug of testing only makes us feel the security of our Anchor, Christ Jesus. "Knowing this, that the trying of your faith worketh patience" (James 1:3). Tested faith also is precious, and brings praise and honor: "That the trial of your faith, being much more precious than of gold that perisheth, though it be tried with fire, might be found unto praise and honor and glory at the appearing of Jesus Christ" (I Pet. 1:7).

It is not the *quantity* but the *quality* of faith that counts. When the disciples asked Jesus to increase their faith, He told them that if they had faith no bigger than a mustard seed, they could pluck up a tree by the roots and plant it in the sea (Luke 17:5, 6). It is not the *amount* but the *kind* of faith that matters. A person's faith might be bulky enough to remove mountains, yet without love such a demonstration would mean nothing (I Cor. 13:2). It has the quantity, the amount, but not the quality, the kind of faith required. If our faith is a living germ, born of confidence in God, nurtured by the Spirit, and watered by the Word, it will produce results.

How to Get Faith

Faith is a grace from God in which the whole Trinity is involved.

(1) Faith is God's gift: This is inferred from the fact that Jesus Christ and the Father are one (John

10:30), and that no man comes to Jesus Christ "except the Father ... draw him" (John 6:44). Moreover, there is a "measure of faith" which God has dealt to each Christian (Rom. 12:3).

(2) Faith is one aspect of the fruit of the Spirit: "But the fruit of the Spirit is ... faith" (Gal. 5:22).

(3) Jesus Christ is the Author and Finisher of our faith (Heb. 12:2).

The fact that faith is God's gift does not mean, however, that we are to wait passively and expect something that we call faith to drop from heaven upon us. Just as sunshine is God's gift, but the plant must be exposed to it in order to receive its benefits, so we must expose ourselves to God's Word: "So then faith cometh by hearing, and hearing by the word of God" (Rom. 10:17). In the days of the apostles it was those who heard the Word of God who believed (see Acts 4:4). It was the reception of the Word preached that caused faith to germinate. Like Abraham, we must fix our eyes on the promise of God in order to exercise faith in Him (see Rom. 4:19, 20).

How to Maintain Faith

Faith is the Christian's blood stream. When it stops flowing, spiritual death follows. Faith is as vital to spiritual life as air is to physical life. "The just shall live by faith." This text, given to Habakkuk in the Old Testament (Hab. 2:4), is repeated three times in the New Testament (Rom. 1:17; Gal. 3:11; Heb. 10:38).

We are told to "continue in the faith grounded and settled" (Col. 1:23). We must close our ear to all doubts of God's love for us, and His ability to work for us. We continue in the faith by choosing continually to trust Him.

We are given the shield of faith as part of our armor. We must use it when Satan's fiery darts of unbelief, perplexity, or fear assail us. The fact that we are living a life of faith does not mean we are living a life of apathy. The faith life is a very active, positive one. "Above all, taking the shield of faith, wherewith ye shall be able to quench all the fiery darts of the wicked" (Eph. 6:16).

To maintain faith we must be watchful and not waver. This is not a watchfulness of suspense and fear, but of trust. It is not a scrutiny of ourselves to see how much or how little faith we have, but a watchfulness to see God work as we commit ourselves and our circumstances to Him. We simply stand as sentinels knowing that we are not appointed to fight the enemy singlehanded, but to signal our Captain. The regiments of heaven await the cry of faith coming from the alert watcher. "Watch ye, stand fast in the faith, quit you like men, be strong" (I Cor. 16:13). The life of faith demands the highest type of virile Christianity. It is a privilege to "stand fast in the faith" because Jesus Christ is standing with and for us.

To maintain faith we must keep moving. Like a boy riding a bicycle, we must not stop lest we fall. We must make faith our choice and pursuit if we would live a life of faith. "But thou, man of God, ...

follow after . . . faith" (I Tim. 6:11). "Flee also youthful lusts, but follow . . . faith" (II Tim. 2:22).

The Relationships of Faith

Since faith is essential to spiritual life, it is related to every other Christian experience. Like the blood, which is carried to all parts of a healthy body, so faith reaches every extremity of our spiritual well-being.

Faith is related to repentance, for the latter leads us to faith in Christ (Acts 20:21).

Faith is related to justification; we are justified by faith (Rom. 5:1).

Faith is related to the gospel. The gospel is "the power of God unto salvation to every one that *believeth*" (Rom. 1:16).

Faith is related to the written Word: "But these are *written*, that ye might *believe* . . ." (John 20:31). "These things have I written unto you . . . that ye may *know* that ye have eternal life, and that ye may *believe* on the name of the Son of God" (I John 5:13).

Faith is related to obedience. Unless God has our will, He does not have our faith in Him. "But now [the gospel] is . . . made known to all nations for the *obedience of faith*" (Rom. 16:26).

Faith is related to prayer. There is no such thing as unbelieving prayer, for an utterance made in unbelief is not prayer, and does not gain God's attention unless it is made as a confession of our unbelief and a plea that He will help it: "But without faith it is impossible to please him; for he that cometh to God *must believe that he is, and that he is a rewarder* of them that diligently seek him" (Heb. 11:6). If we want to have our prayers answered, we must believe that God will answer and has answered them: "Therefore I say unto you, All things whatsoever ye pray and ask for, believe that ye received them, and ye shall have them" (Mark 11:24, A.R.V. m.).

Faith is related to works. The familiar passage in James (2:14–26) is not minimizing faith but emphasizing the right kind of faith, the faith that is proved by its works, the faith that has life: "For as the body without the spirit is dead, so faith without works is dead also."

The Effects of Faith

The exploits of faith are limitless. Faith uproots sycamore trees, removes mountains, and brings all things within the realm of possibility: "And the Lord said, If ye had faith as a grain of mustard seed, ye might say unto this sycamine tree, Be thou plucked up by the root, and be thou planted in the sea; and it should obey you" (Luke 17:6). "If ye have faith as a grain of mustard seed, ye shall say unto this mountain, Remove hence to yonder place; and it shall remove; and nothing shall be impossible unto you" (Matt. 17:20).

The list of accomplishments in Hebrews 11 only confirms this. Through faith kingdoms were leveled, lions ceased to roar, fire was quenched, the sword lost its edge, weakness became strength, and armies fled. Some saw death give way before it, and others received grace to suffer (Heb. 11:33–39).

Faith brings us remission of sins: "To him give all the prophets witness, that through his name whosoever believeth in him shall receive remission of sins" (Acts 10:43).

Faith in Christ's atonement work brings us justification: "Therefore being justified by faith, we have peace with God through our Lord Jesus Christ" (Rom. 5:1).

Faith robes us in God's righteousness: "And be found in him, not having mine own righteousness ..., but that which is through faith of Christ, the righteousness which is of God by faith" (Phil. 3:9).

It is by faith we receive the Holy Spirit: "That we might receive the promise of the Spirit through faith" (Gal. 3:14).

It is by faith that Christ's indwelling is maintained: "That Christ may dwell in your hearts by faith" (Eph. 3:17).

Anything less than faith makes us spiritual paupers, but through faith we partake of the "unsearchable riches of Christ" (Eph. 3:8).

CHAPTER THREE

CONVERSION

Definition of Conversion

Christian conversion is that act whereby one turns from sin to Christ Jesus for both his forgiveness of sins and his salvation from them. This includes deliverance from the penalty of sin. Conversion, though closely allied to repentance, is different from it in that repentance emphasizes the negative aspect of turning *from* sin, and conversion emphasizes the positive aspect of turning *to* Christ. Repentance turns us *from* all other lovers; conversion turns us *to* the Bridegroom. Repentance produces sorrow for sin; conversion produces joy because of forgiveness and deliverance from sin's penalty. Repentance brings us to the cross; conversion brings us to the empty tomb and the risen Saviour.

Christian conversion should be distinguished from other kinds of conversion. The word "conversion" literally means "to twist" or turn quite around. In this literal sense, therefore, one can be converted from one view to another. He can change his political party, and thus be converted politically. He can change from one denomination to another, and thus be converted religiously. As we advance in knowledge and maturity, we continually become converted from former childish views to more accurate ones. You no longer believe that the universe revolves around your home town, nor that the stars are holes in the sky. Thus we are converted mentally. "When I was a child, I spake as a child, I understood as a child, I thought as a child" (I Cor. 13:11). A child can be taught that it is wrong to pick up toys from the department store counter, or to scratch the faces of other youngsters, or to interrupt the conversation of adults. Thus he becomes converted ethically.

One can be converted from one preacher to another. The Corinthian church was divided. Some followed Paul, others Apollos, others Cephas (Peter) and others—as they claimed—Christ (I Cor. 1:12). The trouble is that one is likely to consider a person a born-again Christian who is merely a convert to some denomination, or to some evangelist, or to some religious philosophy, even a fundamental one. Such a convert has only changed one coat of paint for another. A Christian convert has a change of nature.

Conversion can be *mental* only. When one changes his views, he has become mentally converted.

Conversion can be *moral* only. To live a moral life is commendable, but morality is no passport to heaven. The rich young ruler, with all his morality, knew that he lacked something yet, and wanted to know what to do to gain eternal life (Mark 10:17-22). One can be delivered from alcoholism, but not from sin. One can give up certain forms of worldly amusement for the sake of influence or because of circumstances that prevent participation in them, and yet retain the desire to do them. Lot's wife was forced out of Sodom, but Sodom never got out of her. A conversion that is nothing but outward conformity to certain standards that we know we are expected to live up to is not Christian conversion. A candy apple tied on a Christmas tree is not a fruit of that tree. It takes an apple tree to produce apples.

Christian conversion is a *spiritual* change that involves one both mentally and morally. It affects the will. It means a change of desire. It is a heart conviction that changes one's whole outlook and course of action.

Use of the Word Conversion in the Bible

Conversion can be applied to inanimate things. "The abundance of the sea shall be converted unto thee" (Isa. 60:5). Here the lifeless sea is spoken of as being converted, or turned.

In David's penitential prayer he declares, "Sinners shall be converted unto thee" (Psa. 51:13). Here a different word is used, carrying the idea of returning to the starting point. When one is converted *to God* and not to man, he has come back to God's original purpose for him. This verse illustrates both moral and spiritual conversion.

When Jesus said to Peter, "When thou art converted, strengthen the brethren" (Luke 22:32), He did not mean that Peter was not spiritually converted, for Peter was an ardent follower of his Master. Jesus was predicting Peter's failure in denying Him, and declared He had prayed for him that his faith would not fail. Peter's "conversion," therefore, was a turning from his backslidden condition, from his protection of self to renunciation of the self-life. This "conversion" qualified him to help others who might be in similar jeopardy.

The admonition to be converted and become as little children (Matt. 18:3), refers to a spiritual change. It takes a change on the inside to make us childlike enough to receive the gospel and follow Jesus. The openness of a child, the sincere trust of a child, the submissiveness of a child are all characteristics of one who is converted to Christ.

Again in Mark 4:12 a spiritual change is referred to: "Lest at any time they should be converted, and their sins should be forgiven them." Here forgiveness of sins and conversion are tied together. Christian conversion always includes such forgiveness. It is one thing to be forgiven of man, but another to be forgiven of God. To be forgiven of men is human and proper, and we who need forgiveness of men should forgive men. But to be forgiven of God is divine, for God is in no way obligated to men. They have rebelled against Him and spurned His commandments. To be forgiven of Him is one of man's highest benefits, and it is received by trusting in the merits of man's Substitute, Christ Jesus, God's Son.

In Acts 3:19 the relation of repentance to conversion is revealed: "Repent ye therefore, and be converted, that your sins may be blotted out." This verse seems to explain the normal order: first repentance, then conversion, resulting in the blotting out of one's sins.

The Means of Conversion

The Scriptures present both the human and the divine sides of conversion. God calls on men to turn to Him. "Turn you at my reproof" (Prov. 1:23). "Turn ye unto him from whom the children of Israel have deeply revolted" (Isa. 31:6). "And the Redeemer shall come to Zion, and unto them that turn from transgression in Jacob, saith the LORD" (Isa. 59:20). "For I have no pleasure in the death of him that dieth, saith the Lord GOD: wherefore turn yourselves, and live ye" (Ezek. 18:32). "Therefore turn thou to thy God" (Hos. 12:6). "Turn ye even to me with all your heart . . . ; turn unto the Lord your God" (Joel 2:12, 13). Paul in his preaching "shewed . . . to the Gentiles that they should repent and turn to God" (Acts 26:20).

God always respects the human will. When He created man and gave him his high endowment of personality, He made a creature that could either defy and turn from Him, or choose and turn to Him. On the other hand, it is God who turns men to himself. The Psalmist prayed, "Turn us, O God of our salvation, and cause thine anger toward us to cease" (Psa. 85:4). This is the divine side of conversion. The prophet expressed the same petition: "Turn thou me, and I shall be turned; for thou art the LORD my God" (Jer. 31:18b). "Turn thou us unto thee, O LORD, and we shall be turned; renew our days as of old" (Lam. 5:21).

It is possible to recognize both the human and divine side in conversion without belittling man's free will or infringing upon God's sovereignty. To see only the human side is to make God a puppet, subject to the caprice of man and his will. To see only the divine side is to make man a pawn on a chessboard, irresponsible for his actions and incapable of choice. Man's free will is by no means eclipsed by God's sovereignty when we remember that it was God himself who chose to make such a creature, and that the functions of human will are within the limitations of the divine decree. God's sovereignty is not robbed of any of its majesty when we remember that His appeal is always to man's will, and that for such a creature voluntarily to choose God only brings further glory to God, and enhances that sovereignty which has allowed to man the power of choice.

When man turns to God, he simply allows God to step over the threshold and take control (see Rev. 3:20). When God steps in, He turns man in the new course. Man is like a child at the steering wheel, unable to control the ruinous course. When he turns to God, he allows Him to take the wheel. Thus, man turns to God; and God turns man in the way of righteousness. It is quite proper, therefore, for us to appeal to God to turn us. It is just as proper for God to appeal to us to turn.

It is by the *preaching of the gospel* that men turn to God and that God turns men. According to Paul's own testimony, his commission from God to the Gentiles was "to open their eyes, and turn them from darkness to light, and from the power of Satan unto

God, that they may receive forgiveness of sins, and inheritance among them which are sanctified by faith that is in me [Jesus]" (Acts 26:18). He carried this heavenly vision into execution by preaching at once in Damascus, and then by expanding his preaching throughout the Gentile world (Acts 26:20).

The Candidates for Conversion

Since conversion means to turn, *those going in the wrong direction* are called upon to turn. This includes all, for "all have sinned."

The ones who are called of God will turn. There is, according to theologians, both a general and special call of God. The general call is to "whosoever"; the special call is to those who respond. The general call is to the whole world; the special call is to those who have been chosen in Him "before the foundation of the world" (Eph. 1:4). The general call is for those whom God wants, for He "will have all men to be saved, and to come to a knowledge of the truth" (I Tim. 2:4); the special call is for those who want Him. There are many persons still saying, "I pray thee have me excused" (Luke 14:18, 19), but there are still those who are saying, "Lord, remember me" (Luke 23:42). Christ receives those who thus turn, for He is "not willing that any should perish" (II Pet. 3:9). From the divine side, "All that the Father giveth me shall come to me." From the human side, "Him that cometh to me I will in no wise cast out" (John 6:37).

Predestination is in the hands of the omniscient God, and is in conformity with His foreknowledge of the free acts of men. "For whom he did foreknow, he also did predestinate to be conformed to the image of his Son, that he might be the firstborn among many brethren" (Rom. 8:29). A look at Calvary removes all question concerning God's love for the world (John 3:16) and His desire that men turn in faith to the One who was sacrificed for them there. Man settles his own destiny according to his rejection or acceptance of God's Son. Anyone is a candidate for conversion who wants God sincerely enough to call upon Christ Jesus for salvation, for Christ "died for all" (II Cor. 5:15). The question for each of us to settle is not "Am I candidate?" but "What have I done with Jesus?"

The Purpose of Conversion

Negatively, conversion is to turn us from death: "Turn ye, turn ye, from your evil ways; for why will ye die?" (Ezek. 33:11). Conversion is also to save us from ultimate destruction: "Enter ye in at the strait gate: for wide is the gate, and broad is the way that leadeth to destruction" (Matt. 7:13).

Positively, conversion turns us from the broad way to the narrow way that leads to life (Matt. 7:14). The will is captured and used toward righteous ends and a worthy goal.

Conversion also makes our walk and outward life conform to our profession. Our *standing* in Christ becomes a testimony to others because our *state* of Christian living conforms thereto. This does not mean that we have become static and have ceased to advance. We are continually being transformed into God's image; we are facing upward, and God's image is being reflected by us to others (II Cor. 3:18). A professing Christian who lives no differently from the world is so opaque that there is no reflection of God's glory and no testimony for Christ.

Conversion gives us a testimony to both God and man. We become living epistles (II Cor. 3:2) conveying God's message to men. We give feet to the gospel of Christ by the way we walk.

The Results of Conversion

One of the first results of conversion is *salvation from death*: "He that converteth a sinner from the error of his way shall save a soul from death, and shall hide a multitude of sins" (James 5:20). This refers to the second death, which is the lake of fire: "And death and hell were cast into the lake of fire. This is the second death" (Rev. 20:14). This is the terminus of the broad way: "And whosoever was not found written in the book of life was cast into the lake of fire" (Rev. 20:15). Conversion turns us from the broad way ending in eternal torment to the narrow way ending in eternal life, which eternal life we now have through faith in Christ (John 3:16). Simple faith in Christ places our name in the Book of Life and gives us eternal life now, to be consummated at the coming of Christ for His Church. "And this is the record, that God hath given to us eternal life, and this life is in his Son. He that hath the Son hath life; and he that hath not the Son of God hath not life" (I John 5:11, 12). Have you received the Son of God and eternal life?

Another result is that *our sins are blotted out*: "Repent ye therefore, and be converted, that your sins may be blotted out" (Acts 3:19). There is a difference between having our sins concealed and having them blotted out. The first is to try to hide them by burying them. But the evil seed will spring up again and expose the concealment. The second is to have them removed as far as the east is from the west (Psa. 103:12) and expunged from God's memory. "I, even I, am he that blotteth out thy transgressions for mine own sake, and will not remember thy sins" (Isa. 43:25).

Conversion also brings us *spiritual healing* (see Acts 28:27). To turn from Christ is to turn from the one true remedy for the soul. The good Samaritan pours oil and wine into our wounds, and gently leads us to the inn for soul healing (Luke 10:34).

Conversion brings us into *fellowship*. "God is faithful, by whom ye were called unto the fellowship of his Son Jesus Christ our Lord" (I Cor. 1:9). Our first call is to fellowship with Jesus Christ. This takes precedence over the call to service, or any other call. There can be no fellowship between righteousness and unrighteousness, light and darkness, Christ and Belial, a believer and unbeliever, the worship of God and idolatry (II Cor. 6:14-16). When we are converted, our relationships are entirely different: "And truly our fellowship is with the Father, and with his Son Jesus Christ" (I John 1:3b). Conversion is no sacrifice to the one who has exchanged the pig pen for the palace, his rags for the robe, the road into the far country for the arms of the waiting Father. Nor is conversion anything but complete gain to the self-righteous culprit who finds "the righteousness of God" through Christ Jesus (II Cor. 5:21) and the peace that comes through justification by faith (Rom. 5:1).

CHAPTER FOUR

REGENERATION

Definition of Regeneration

Regeneration is that supernatural and instantaneous change wrought by the Holy Spirit in the nature of the individual who receives the Lord Jesus Christ. It is not an evolutionary change, but a revolutionary one. This is described by Jesus as being born again, or from above (see John 3:3–8). Jesus also described it as passing from death into life, a transaction that takes place not in the future but now: "Verily, verily, I say unto you, He that heareth my word, and believeth him that sent me, hath eternal life, and cometh not into judgment, but hath passed out of death into life" (John 5:24, A.R.V.). It also is described as being made a new creature: "Therefore if any man be in Christ, he is a new creature" (II Cor. 5:17). "For in Christ Jesus neither circumcision availeth any thing, nor uncircumcision, but a new creature" (Gal. 6:15).

Regeneration and Reformation

Regeneration is not reformation. Reformation is on the human plane; regeneration, on the divine.

Reformation is something that is attached to the outside; regeneration is a change from within.

Reformation affects the conduct without changing the character; regeneration affects the conduct by changing the character.

Reformation is an acquisition; regeneration is a transformation.

Reformation is an endeavor; regeneration is a new life.

Reformation is an attainment, which many persons think will get them into the kingdom of God; regeneration is a requirement for entering that kingdom (John 3:3).

Reformation is the outcome of self-effort, but it does not deal with the basic problems of sin and death; regeneration is the result of a new law that liberates us. "For the law of the Spirit of life in Christ Jesus hath made me free from the law of sin and death" (Rom. 8:2).

The Meaning of Regeneration

The word "regeneration" (paliggenesia) literally means "a birth again," a new birth. It refers to a renovation, a renewal, a restoration, a re-creation. It occurs only twice in the Bible: (1) "Verily I say unto you, That ye which have followed me, in the regeneration when the Son of man shall sit in the throne of his glory, ye also shall sit upon twelve thrones, judging the twelve tribes of Israel" (Matt. 19:28). Here the word refers to the future day of Christ's reign. (2) "Not by works of righteousness which we have done, but according to his mercy he saved us, by the washing of regeneration, and renewing of the Holy Ghost" (Tit. 3:5). Here the word refers to the work of the new birth. Though this word is used but twice, the experience is described by various titles. It takes more than one word to tell the wonder and mystery of this work.

This superb work is unparalleled in any other philosophy. All religions outside Christianity are trying to climb up to God. The serpent's hiss, "Ye shall be as gods" (Gen. 3:5), is in their teaching. But in Christ Jesus, God comes down to man, reaches him at the lowest depths of his degradation, quickens him into spiritual life, and raises him into a new sphere. "And you hath he quickened, who were dead in trespasses and sins.... But God, who is rich in mercy ..., hath quickened us together with Christ, ... and hath raised us up together, and made us sit together in heavenly places in Christ Jesus" (Eph. 2:1, 4–6). How amazing that any one would not accept such an overture!

The Necessity for Regeneration

The necessity for regeneration lies in man. When the theologians speak of man's *total depravity*, they do not mean that all men are as low as they possibly can be. Some are born with greater handicaps than others. Some are reared in an environment of filth and moral uncleanness; others, amidst culture and refinement. Some are born in paganism with its low and degrading standards and practices; others are born in Christian lands where a mere twist of the dial will bring them a gospel program. Some have a genealogical background of crime and base living; others can num-

58

ber preachers, educators, and other professional men among their ancestors.

Total depravity means that every part of man's being—spirit, soul, and body—has been affected by the fall of our first parent, Adam: "Wherefore, as by one man sin entered into the world, and death by sin; and so death passed upon all men, for that all have sinned" (Rom. 5:12). "There is none righteous, no, not one" (Rom. 3:10). "For all have sinned, and come short of the glory of God" (Rom. 3:23). If a drop of poison is put into a glass of water, the whole is poisoned, not just a part of it. The virus of sin entered the human blood stream when man fell, and every part of his being has become tainted.

Spiritually, man is *dead*. The spirit of man is like the top story, with a skylight that opens to heaven. When Adam fell, this part of his being died at once. He had a blackout. That is why, when God came down to the garden, Adam ran to hide. There was no spiritual response to God-fellowship. There was fear instead. This dreadful tragedy was passed on to Adam's entire posterity.

This spiritually dead condition is also described as the "old man." Here are his traits: "anger, wrath, malice, blasphemy, filthy communication out of your mouth. Lie not one to another, seeing that ye have put off the old man with his deeds" (Col. 3:8, 9).

There is nothing in man that is capable of spiritual fellowship with God. Mankind is "carnal, sold under sin" (Rom. 7:14). In him "dwelleth no good thing" (Rom. 7:18). He is "dead in trespasses and sins"— with the consequence that he walks "according to the course of this world, according to the prince of the power of the air, the spirit that now worketh in the children of disobedience," and his manner of life follows "the lusts of our flesh, fulfilling the desires of the flesh and of the mind," and he is by nature a child "of wrath" (Eph. 2:1–3). Note that to fulfill the desires "of the mind" puts one in the category of spiritual death just as much as to fulfill the "lusts of our flesh." In other words, self-centeredness betrays us as being dead to God.

Intellectually, man is affected by the Fall. This is not to ignore the high achievements of man in science, philosophy, and the arts. But no matter how high man advances mentally, he is still dead to the things of God. "But the natural man receiveth not the things of the Spirit of God: for they are foolishness unto him: neither can he know them, because they are spiritually discerned" (I Cor. 2:14). The best educated men that the human race has ever produced, if they are not born again spiritually, still have "the understanding darkened, being alienated from the life of God through the ignorance that is in them, because of the blindness of their heart" (Eph. 4:18). Nicodemus was "*the* teacher in Israel" (John 3:10, A.R.V.), evidently a renowned educational leader. Yet Jesus frankly faced him with the stark fact: "If I have told you earthly things, and ye believe not, how shall ye believe, if I tell you of heavenly things?" (John 3:12). The reason for this density is obvious.

Nicodemus, as Jesus said, had to be born from above. Education never takes a man higher than the top of his skull. Beyond that he needs a divine work from a higher sphere if he would enter that sphere. He must be regenerated, born anew.

Physically, too, man is affected by the Fall. Sickness, disease, and death have all moved in. "And he died" is the epitaph written on every tombstone in the graveyard of Genesis 5, with the single exception of Enoch. Death took the throne and reigned at once, even before the law was given: "Nevertheless death reigned from Adam to Moses, even over them that had not sinned after the similitude of Adam's transgression" (Rom. 5:14). The reason is that sin brought death into the race: "Wherefore, as by one man sin entered into the world, and death by sin; and so death passed upon all men, for that all have sinned" (Rom. 5:12). In spite of the arduous endeavor to combat disease, men continue to die.

God's verdict is unmistakable. Sin has tainted man in every part of his being. "There is none righteous, no, not one: there is none that understandeth, there is none that seeketh after God . . . , there is none that doeth good, no, not one" (Rom. 3:10–12). Regeneration is an unequivocal *must* for a creature in such a condition as this.

The Means of Regeneration

Regeneration does not come by living a *good life*. Morality is an evidence and fruit of regeneration, but not the root. One who is regenerated will live a good life because his nature has been changed. The Ethiopian cannot change his skin nor the leopard his spots (Jer. 13:23) except by a change on the inside. Some persons wear a coat of morality, which is nothing but a coverup. When good works and good living are produced by a change of nature, they are permanent and effective.

Education will not regenerate the life. It will enlighten the intellect and enlarge the outlook and correct many false notions and practices, but it will not bring us in touch with God. One can be highly educated and extremely conceited. "Knowledge puffeth up" (I Cor. 8:1). Whatever knowledge the Christian gains should be held in "meekness of wisdom" (James 3:13). God works above and beyond the wisdom of this world: "Where is the wise? where is the scribe? where is the disputer of this world? hath not God made foolish the wisdom of this world? For after that in the wisdom of God the world by wisdom knew not God, it pleased God by the foolishness of preaching to save them that believe" (I Cor. 1:20, 21).

If education were the means of regeneration, then that gracious work would be unattainable for many persons. But God has put regeneration within the reach of all men.

Church membership will not regenerate us. It is one thing to have the name written on a church register, and another to have it in the Lamb's book of life. Christians should identify themselves with some body of believers, and church membership is a worthy means of propagating Christian fellowship and the spreading of the gospel, but one who has his name written in a record on earth should also have it written in heaven. Otherwise he is nothing but an adherent to an institution, and knows nothing of spiritual vitality as a member of the body of Christ.

Baptism does not regenerate. There is no inherent value in water itself. A bath, which Peter calls "a putting away of the filth of the flesh," has no potency to reach the evil heart of the unregenerated. When baptism is "the answer of a good conscience toward God," when the baptismal candidate puts his trust in the resurrected Christ as his Saviour (I Pet. 3:21), then this sacred ordinance has its proper testimony. Baptism is a holy rite practiced by believers. It is a declaration to God, to the candidate himself, and to the world that the one participating therein is identifying himself with Christ's death and resurrection, and has become a humble follower of the Lamb. "Therefore we are buried with him by baptism into death: that like as Christ was raised up from the dead by the glory of the Father, even so we also should walk in newness of life" (Rom. 6:4).

Religious ceremonies will not produce regeneration. Non-Christian religions have forms of prayer, ablutions, ritualistic observances, yet the votaries know nothing of a changed life or deliverance from sin. It is possible for one to go through all the forms that his church or creed demands, and still be unregenerated. To substitute formalism for personal faith in Christ Jesus is to set aside His work on the cross.

There are *both the human and divine sides* in
the work of regeneration. It is true that *God alone
regenerates;* the work is absolutely divine, and comes
from above. But it is also true that *there is a responsibility* resting upon those who know the Saviour to
preach Him to others (Rom. 10:14; I Cor. 1:21), and
to pray (Matt. 9:38; Rom. 10:1). The responsibility
resting on the unregenerated is to respond to God's
invitation.

One of the first hindrances to man's regeneration
is his pride. This enemy stands guard to turn back
all offers of mercy that come to man. Consequently,
one of the first requisites is that one must become as
a little child: "Verily I say unto you, Whosoever
shall not receive the kingdom of God as a little child
shall in no wise enter therein" (Luke 18:17). The
way is narrow that leads to life, and only those who
are willing to humble themselves are able to enter
therein.

Regeneration comes through *believing God's written
Word*: "These things have I written unto you that
believe on the name of the Son of God; that ye may
know that ye have eternal life, and that ye may believe
on the name of the Son of God" (I John 5:13).

To believe the Word is to believe the record concerning Jesus, and to rest not only on the Word but
also upon Jesus himself whom the Word reveals:
"And this is the record, that God hath given to us
eternal life, and this life is in his Son. He that hath
the Son hath life" (I John 5:11, 12a).

To believe God's record in His Word means more than an intellectual assent thereto. The believing that saves must come from the heart; that is, the whole being—will, emotions, reasonings—must cooperate: "That if thou shalt confess with thy mouth the Lord Jesus, and shalt believe in thine heart that God hath raised him from the dead, thou shalt be saved. For with the heart man believeth unto righteousness; and with the mouth confession is made unto salvation" (Rom. 10:9, 10).

Regeneration comes through *receiving Jesus Christ*. This involves the will. Christ does not force the door open: "Behold, I stand at the door and knock: if any man hear my voice, and open the door, I will come in to him, and will sup with him, and he with me" (Rev. 3:20). Receiving Jesus is an act of faith: "But as many as received him, to them gave he power to become the sons of God, even to them that believe on his name" (John 1:12).

As to the *divine side of regeneration* this comes directly from God. It is *of God* that the believer is born again: "Which were born, not of blood, nor of the will of the flesh, nor of the will of man, but of God" (John 1:13). This is known also as the birth *by the Spirit*: "That which is born of the flesh is flesh; and that which is born of the Spirit is spirit" (John 3:6). It is also the "washing of regeneration and renewing of the Holy Ghost" (Titus 3:5). It is by the Spirit that *Christ enters* the opened door of the heart, and makes His abode there (Rev. 3:20). Thus the Trinity combine in producing regeneration.

65

God uses His Word as an agent in the work of regeneration: "Of his own will begat he us with the word of truth, that we should be a kind of firstfruits of his creatures" (James 1:18). "Being born again, not of corruptible seed, but of incorruptible, by the word of God, which liveth and abideth for ever" (I Pet. 1:23). Those who would work with God in the salvation of souls must therefore preach the Word, for this is God's means.

In the final analysis, regeneration is a mystery, but nonetheless a reality: "The wind bloweth where it listeth, and thou hearest the sound thereof, but canst not tell whence it cometh, and whither it goeth: so is every one that is born of the Spirit" (John 3:8). We can see the effects but cannot explain the operation, though we can experience it.

The Evidence of Regeneration

One of the first evidences negatively is that the regenerated one *escapes the corruption that is in the world* because a new nature has been implanted within him: "Whereby are given unto us exceeding great and precious promises: that by these ye might be partakers of the divine nature, having escaped the corruption that is in the world through lust" (II Pet. 1:4). The *positive* correlative of this is that he overcomes the world: "For whosoever is born of God overcometh the world" (I John 5:4):

Negatively, too, the regenerated one is *delivered from the practice of sin*. If he does commit sin as a single act, he appeals to his Advocate, Christ Jesus, and to the cleansing blood (I John 2:1, 2; 1:9), but he has quit committing sin as a practice: "Whosoever hath been born of God is not committing sin" (I John 3:9, Rotherham). On the *positive* side, he practices righteousness: "Every one that doeth righteousness is born of him" (I John 2:29b). The old habits are replaced by new habits of righteousness.

The regenerated one *loves God*. This is not a love of the emotions only, but also of the will, changing the center of interest from self to God: "The love of God is shed abroad in our hearts by the Holy Ghost which is given unto us" (Rom. 5:5b). "We love him because he first loved us" (I John 4:19).

Love to God automatically has *love to the brethren* as its yokefellow: "By this we know that we love the children of God, when we love God, and keep his commandments" (I John 5:2). Love to the brethren is a practical evidence of our love to God: "For he that loveth not his brother whom he hath seen, how can he love God whom he hath not seen?" (I John 4:20). "We know that we have passed from death unto life, because we love the brethren" (I John 3:14). This evidence of love to the brother assures us as well as our brother of the fact of our regeneration.

The Climax of Regeneration

When God regenerates a person, He works according to a pattern, and that pattern is Jesus Christ. Christlikeness is the goal for every born-again child of God. "Beloved, now are we the sons of God, and it doth not yet appear what we shall be: but we know that when he shall appear, we shall be like him; for we shall see him as he is" (I John 3:2). This is nothing short of conformity to the image of the Son of God.

This does not mean that our transformation to Christlikeness is being postponed till the day He appears. If the hope of His appearing is real to us, we are purifying ourselves in view of that wonderful day (I John 3:3).

The means of this transformation is by keeping our eyes upon Christ Jesus; thereby we are changed: "But we all, with open face beholding as in a glass the glory of the Lord, are changed into the same image from glory to glory, even as by the Spirit of the Lord" (II Cor. 3:18).

The climax of our regeneration is glorification: "For whom he did foreknow, he also did predestinate to be conformed to the image of his Son. . . . Moreover whom he did predestinate, them he also called: and whom he called, them he also justified: and whom he justified, them he also glorified" (Rom. 8:29, 30).

The work of regeneration comes from above, and proceeds according to this heavenly pattern. Regeneration is divine from start to finish.

CHAPTER FIVE

JUSTIFICATION

Definition of Justification

Justification is that act of God's grace whereby He declares righteous the person who places faith in Jesus Christ as his Substitute and Saviour.

While it is true that the word "justification" means "to make righteous," yet according to usage it means to pronounce or declare righteous. It is therefore an objective work, that is, it takes place outside of us at God's throne.

The Meaning of Justification

Justification is not a judicial act, for the law cannot justify the sinner; it can only condemn him. But it is an act of grace based on the finished work of Christ. The person declared righteous is thereby declared free from guilt and punishment.

Justification is not the same as forgiveness or pardon. A criminal may be pardoned by the governor, but he does not leave behind him in his cell the guilt that rested upon him; he carries that guilt with him out into his freedom. He has been forgiven but not exonerated since he was actually guilty of the crime for which he was imprisoned. But in the case of one who is justified, he is exonerated, not because he does not deserve punishment and not because he no longer carries the memory of his guilt, but because the law's demands have been satisfied. Another has taken his place and suffered his execution. The law has no claim upon him.

Justification is not the same as declaring one innocent, for such a declaration would be untrue. God can treat us as though we had never sinned, not because we are innocent, but because the righteousness of His Son has been put to our account. Christ is made unto us righteousness (I Cor. 1:30). Many a man who has been pardoned by men has still suffered under the reproach of his former prison record. But it is far different with the man whom God justifies. What an unspeakable benediction rests on the soul that can step out of his prison cell of sin and guilt and deserved penalty into the free air of justification without a twinge of fear because of the law. God is satisfied, grace is magnified, and the sinner is justified.

Justification and the Law

There are three reasons why the law cannot justify us. First, the law is "weak through the flesh" (Rom. 8:3)—that is, the law has power to diagnose our disease called sin, but no power to effect a cure. It can, like a mirror, reveal to us our uncleanness, but it cannot wash it away. No amount of gazing into a mirror will wash a dirty face. The law holds up to us God's standard of holiness and shows us our shortcomings, but it cannot lift us up. Like the priest and Levite who left to his fate the man victimized by robbers on the Jericho road, the law leaves us helpless. It has no power to recover us of our condition. It takes the Good Samaritan to do that.

The second reason why the law cannot justify is that the law knows no mercy. It is rigid. In order to be justified by the law one must keep it perfectly. The man who thinks he can keep the law is like a drunken tight-rope walker attempting to bridge a deep chasm. The fallen nature of man cannot possibly perform such a feat. Even a cursory reading of man's record in the Scriptures will make evident how many tumbles he has had. Consequently, the law, instead of bringing a blessing, brings a curse: "For as many as are of the works of the law are under the curse: for it is written, Cursed is every one that continueth not in all things which are written in the book of the law to do them" (Gal. 3:10).

The third reason is that the law cannot rectify the past nor cleanse the inner sinfulness with which every child of Adam is defiled. Suppose one could turn over a new leaf and start keeping the law flawlessly. The record of his life from then on would be acceptable, but the record before that time would not be. It is the *whole* life, not just the part after turning over the new leaf, that must be rectified before God. Moreover, even though one were able to keep the law perfectly during his whole life, this would not cleanse away the inherent sinfulness of his nature. It was because of this inward need that David prayed God to create in him a clean heart and renew a right spirit within him (Psa. 51:10). Nothing but the blood of Jesus can do this.

In fact, the law was never given to justify any one. It was given "that sin by the commandment might become exceeding sinful" (Rom. 7:13). There is nothing wrong with the law, for "the law is holy, and the commandment holy, and just, and good" (Rom. 7:12). The wrong is with man, and the law discloses that fact. The microscope that reveals germs in polluted water does not produce those germs, but simply shows that they are there.

The law was given to show man his hopeless condition, and the impossibility of his justification apart from Jesus Christ. "For the law was given by Moses, but grace and truth came by Jesus Christ" (John 1:17). Happy hopelessness indeed for the man who sees his condition and turns in faith to Christ.

In summary, the law cannot justify us, "for by the law is the knowledge of sin" (Rom. 3:20). The law cannot bring us salvation, but it does bring us to the Saviour: "Wherefore the law was our schoolmaster to bring us unto Christ, that we might be justified by faith" (Gal. 3:24). The one who thinks he can be justified by living a good life or keeping the law has no idea of the high standard that God's law demands. It is only because Christ Jesus perfectly met this standard and died in our place that God can justify the man who trusts Christ. Justification is an act of God's grace based on Christ's fulfillment of the law. It is made effective by personal faith in the Fulfiller of that law. Calvary is more than an expression of the love and grace of God; it is also an execution of the law's demands. Christ's work on the cross is sufficient for all, but effective for those who believe.

Justification and Regeneration

Justification takes place outside us at the throne of God where He declares us righteous. It is therefore objective.

Regeneration is a divine work wrought inside us. It is therefore subjective.

Justification is God's verdict; regeneration is man's experience.

Justification is what Christ does *for* us; regeneration is what the Holy Spirit does *in* us.

Justification has to do with our *standing;* regeneration, with our *state.*

Justification changes our *relation to God;* regeneration, our *nature.*

Both justification and regeneration must be considered together, for they take place simultaneously, and are two aspects of one work. At the same time that God by His Spirit regenerates us, He also justifies us, declaring us righteous and free from liability to punishment, thus treating us as though we had never sinned. Oh the wonder of salvation through our Lord Jesus Christ!

The Source of Justification

God is the one and only source of justification, for He alone is righteous. Righteousness is one of the seven compound names for Jehovah: "And this is the name whereby he shall be called, THE LORD OUR RIGHTEOUSNESS [Jehovah-tsidkenu]" (Jer. 23:6).

How then can God justify man the sinner, burdened with guilt and under penalty for his sin? If God were to declare such a person righteous and free from both guilt and penalty, He would bring reproach on His own righteous character unless He had a proper basis for said declaration. A god whose character is blemished is no object of either worship or respect. Unless there is a way whereby God can justify sinful man without bringing His own holy character into question, man has no salvation and no God.

The answer is the cross. It is because God set forth Christ Jesus as "a propitiation through faith in his blood" that God can justify the sinner and at the same time be just in so doing. The prime purpose of Calvary is "to declare his [God's] righteousness for the remission of sins" (Rom. 3:24–26). The cross of Christ assures us of more than God's willingness to forgive our sins; it assures us of His justice in forgiving us. "He is faithful and just to forgive us our sins" (I John 1:9). Thus the one who places his faith in the blood of Jesus is justified by the very God whom he can still worship and adore. Calvary is both a protection of God's character and a declaration of it, including both His justice and love. It is also man's only means of approach to God. Thus he can draw near without fear "in full assurance of faith"

(Heb. 10:22) and with unrestrained adoration. "O the depth of the riches both of the wisdom and knowledge of God!" (Rom. 11:33).

The Scriptures therefore properly represent righteousness as coming from God. God states that the righteousness of "the servants of the LORD . . . is of me" (Isa. 45:17b). It is the robe of His righteousness with which the believer is covered (Isa. 61:10).

It is appropriate for the believer to recognize and acknowledge the source of his righteousness. "Surely, shall one say, in the LORD have I righteousness and strength" (Isa. 45:24). "I will make mention of thy righteousness, even of thine only" (Psa. 71:16b).

Justification would be impossible except for the work of Christ. Thus He is the Accomplisher of our justification through voluntarily and vicariously assuming our sin and dying in our place. "The LORD hath laid on him the iniquity of us all" (Isa. 53:6b). Christ Jesus has been called the *meritorious* cause of our justification. "By his knowledge shall my righteous servant justify many; for he shall bear their iniquities" (Isa. 53:11b).

Justification is applicable to all who place faith in the atonement work of Christ Jesus. "Therefore being justified by faith, we have peace with God through our Lord Jesus Christ" (Rom. 5:1).

Thus God is the *originator* of justification, Christ is the *accomplisher* of it, and man through personal faith is the *receiver*.

Scripture Illustrations of Justification

There are two outstanding illustrations of justification found in Romans. David is the first. He illustrates justification by faith *apart from works*. "Even
as David also pronounceth blessing upon the man, unto
whom God reckoneth righteousness apart from works,
saying, Blessed are they whose iniquities are forgiven,
and whose sins are covered. Blessed is the man to whom
the Lord will not reckon sin" (Rom. 4:6–8, A.R.V.).

Note that this is not faith with works absent, but
faith *apart from works*. Works do not come first, but
faith alone. It is the kind of faith, however, that has
works following, as evidence of its quality. There is no
contradiction between this statement in Romans 4 and
the one in James 2:14–26, any more than there is
between the root of a tree and its fruit. Paul writes
of *the root*, which is pure faith apart from works.
James writes of *the fruit*, which proves the kind of
root producing such fruit. It is faith apart from works
that justifies us; but it is not the faith that has no
works, for a faith void of works is void of vitality
(see James 2:26). But at the same time it is not works
that produce faith, but faith that produces works, and
we are justified by the faith that does produce them.

The second illustration is Abraham. He illustrates
justification by faith *apart from ritual*. He was justified
by faith before he was circumcised (Rom. 4:10). Those
who experience justification do not receive it through
the law: "For the promise that he should be heir of
the world, was not to Abraham, or to his seed, through

the law, but through the righteousness of faith" (Rom. 4:13).

To fit into God's pattern one must come as he is, and receive what He gives.

The Extent of Justification

The extent of the atonement of Christ is not the same as the extent of justification. "God so loved *the world*" (John 3:16). The Lamb of God "taketh away the sin of *the world*" (John 1:29). God has laid on His Son "the iniquity of *us all*" (Isa. 53:6). Christ died *for all* (II Cor. 5:14, 15). God's provision is complete.

Justification, however, is only for those who believe. The *provision* for justification is not limited, but the *appropriation* of it is limited to those who will trust that provision.

The Means of Justification

Faith is the means whereby one is justified. But the faith that justifies rests on the finished work of Christ. "And by him all that believe are justified from all things, from which ye could not be justified by the law of Moses" (Acts 13:39). "Therefore we conclude that a man is justified by faith without the deeds of the law" (Rom. 3:28). "For Christ is the end of the law for righteousness to every one that believeth" (Rom. 10:4). We are justified "by the faith of Jesus Christ" (Gal. 2:16). The bridge of faith connects us to all the blessings of justification.

The ship in the canal lock is not lifted by its own power but by the tide. But in order to let the tide come in, the gates must be opened. So it is personal faith that opens the gates and lets God's tide of provision in Christ Jesus lift us to the high level of justification.

The Benefits of Justification

One of the first benefits of justification is that we are "saved from wrath through him" (Rom. 5:9). There are no charges against us. We may therefore humbly yet boldly ask, "Who shall lay anything to the charge of God's elect? Shall God that justifieth?" (Rom. 8:33, A.R.V. m.). The obvious answer is "No." The God who justifies us would not contradict His own work by laying any charges against us at the same time. The haunting fear of judgment is banished by the blessed assurance of acceptance with God.

Another benefit is that the sin question is settled. This fact brings one into the company of the blessed. "Blessed is he whose transgression is forgiven, whose sin is covered" (Psa. 32:1).

Another benefit is peace: "We have peace with God" (Rom. 5:1). Instead of running to hide from God, as Adam did, we draw near, and sit down at the same banquet table, eating with Him, and He with us (Rev. 3:20).

Still another benefit of justification is that we are made heirs. "That being justified by his grace, we should be made heirs according to the hope of eternal life" (Titus 3:7). We are no more servants but sons. God who has taken us into fellowship through justifying us has also taken us into heirship: "Heirs of God, and joint-heirs with Christ" (Rom. 8:17). Such treatment may well amaze us. May it also stimulate us to live for Him alone.

CHAPTER SIX

ADOPTION

Definition of Adoption

Adoption is that act of grace whereby God places as sons those who receive Christ Jesus, bestowing on them all the rights and privileges of sonship.

In the Scriptures the word does not have the same meaning as its ordinary usage in our language. The word "adoption" literally means "the placing of a son."

Regeneration is a change of our nature.

Justification is a change of our standing before God.

Adoption is a change of our rank and position. It has to do with our *privileges* as sons. When we become children of God through receiving Jesus Christ (John 1:12), God does not treat us as servants, nor as children still under tutors and governors, but as those who have received "the adoption of sons" (see Gal. 4:1–5). We are treated as heirs who can draw on the rights of our inheritance.

The Means of Adoption

Man's part in entering into adoption is the same as when he is regenerated and justified, for all three-regeneration, justification, and adoption—are different phases of the great work of man's redemption and reconciliation. Man's part is to believe in Jesus Christ and to receive Him. But this • believing is with the heart; that is, the whole being must respond. It means more than an intellectual assent to the truths of the gospel. "For with the heart man believeth unto righteousness" (Rom. 10:10). And to receive Jesus Christ means a definite act of the will, entailing yielding to Him. It is more than receiving a guest for a social call. It is receiving a Master under whom we take our place as His bondservants. Such believing, and such receiving brings us into sonship: "But as many as received him, to them gave he the power to become the sons of God . . . , which were born, not of blood, nor of the will of the flesh, nor of the will of man, but of God" (John 1:12, 13).

God's part in the work of adoption is sure. Our response to Him gives Him the opportunity He desires. He sends the Spirit of adoption into the heart that has received Jesus Christ: "But ye have received the Spirit of adoption, whereby we cry, Abba, Father" (Rom. 8:15). "And because ye are sons, God hath sent forth the Spirit of his Son into your hearts, crying, Abba, Father" (Gal. 4:6). This form of address, "Abba, Father," was never permitted of slaves; it is the prerogative of sons only. "Abba" is the Hebrew word, and "Father" the Greek. In the family of God there are no racial distinctions; we are one in Christ. "Abba" can be appropriately used by lisping baby lips, and even the most mature cannot cease saying, "Father." Sonship is not a matter of maturity but of birth.

The term "Abba, Father" is first used by Jesus in Gethsemane. When the Spirit of adoption cries out within us, "Abba, Father," it is nothing other than the Spirit of the Son reborn in us, and crying back to His Father. It is the presence of Christ Jesus within, having been received by a definite act of faith, that gives one the power (literally, the authority) to become the son of God. This is the Spirit of life by the new birth. "He that hath the Son hath life; and he that hath not the Son of God hath not life" (I John 5:12). The Spirit of adoption is the Spirit of God's Son within the believing heart.

The Time of Adoption

The time of adoption is unique in that there are three phases. (1) There is the *past* phase of adoption. "According as he hath chosen us in him before the foundation of the world, that we should be holy and without blame before him in love: having predestinated us unto the adoption of children by Jesus Christ to himself, according to the good pleasure of his will" (Eph. 1:4, 5).

Note that God's plan for our adoption reaches back into the past—"before the foundation of the world." Note too that adoption entails not only privilege but also responsibility. As children we are obligated to be holy, and represent our Father by displaying His nature. To this end God predestinated us "that we should be holy and without blame before him in love." To own Him as Father means that He is not ashamed to own us as sons. To experience adoption means far more than a passport to heaven. It means to have the

Spirit of holiness exemplifying *in* us and *through* us the divine nature whereby we have been reborn. Heaven is no place for unclean children, and unclean children are no credit to God upon earth. God's love not only provided His Son to die for us, but also sends the Spirit of that Son within us to make us fit children.

(2) There is the *present* phase of adoption. "Beloved, now are we the sons of God" (I John 3:2). Note the present tense—"Ye *are* sons" (Gal. 4:6). This fact delivers us from apprehensions of the future. We do not wait till we appear before Christ's throne to know whether or not we are His children; we now know that we are sons of God on the authority of His Word and by the Spirit of adoption within us. This fact also presses upon us the obligation of living in this present world as sons of God. God's grace teaches us that "we should live soberly, righteously, and godly, in this present world" (Titus 2:12). Godly living is appropriate for godly children both on earth and in heaven.

(3) There is the *future* phase of adoption. Our experience of adoption has not reached its culmination. We are still subject to physical decay, pain, and death. The outward man "is decaying" (II Cor. 4:16, A.R.V.). We, like all creation, are under the groan of bondage to corruption. "And not only they, but ourselves also, which have the firstfruits of the Spirit, even we ourselves groan within ourselves, waiting for the adoption, to wit, the redemption of our body" (Rom. 8:23). When our adoption is completed, even our bodies will have passed through the metamorphosis of glorification. Those who have died will come forth in resurrected, glorified bodies: "It [the body] is sown in dishonor;

it is raised in glory" (I Cor. 15:43a, also vv. 44-49). Those who remain till the coming of the Lord will be changed without dying: "We shall not all sleep, but we shall all be changed, in a moment, in the twinkling of an eye . . . , for the trumpet shall sound, and the dead shall be raised incorruptible, and we shall be changed" (I Cor. 15:51, 52).

Thus in adoption God's grace reaches from eternity to eternity, lifting us like an infinitesimal particle of dust in the arms of Omnipotence, into a place that angels may well envy. Come, O children of God, and let us glory in our adoption.

The Results of Adoption

First, the Spirit of adoption delivers us from legal bondage. The son of Hagar, the slave, and the son of Sarah, the free woman, cannot live under the same roof (see Gal. 4:21-30). "So then, brethren, we are not children of the bondwoman, but of the free" (Gal. 4:31). God sent His Son for the very purpose of redeeming slaves under the lash of the law, knowing they could do no better, and knowing too that they were suffering the just condemnation of that law. "God sent forth his Son . . . to redeem them that were under the law, that we might receive the adoption of sons" (Gal. 4:4, 5). This place of adoption lifts from our neck the yoke which Peter says "neither our fathers nor we were able to bear" (Acts 15:10). It brings us into the liberty not of sinning but of sonship.

Second, the Spirit of adoption delivers us from fear. Mankind suffers under many fears, some of them warranted, many of them unreal. God's children may suffer under fears—fear of failure; fear of the past, the present, or the future; fear of Satan; fear of man; or fear of self. Such fears are not from God: "God hath not given us the spirit of fear" (II Tim. 1:7). An appropriation of our rights of adoption will deliver us from fear: "For ye have not received the spirit of bondage again to fear; but ye have received the Spirit of adoption . . ." (Rom. 8:15). There is great relief in settling back upon the care of our heavenly Father whose children we are through faith in Jesus Christ. Fear is displaced by filial trust.

Third, the Spirit of adoption brings assurance. "The Spirit itself beareth witness with our spirit, that we are the children of God" (Rom. 8:16). The cry, "Abba, Father," is a true one, inborn by God's own Spirit. This relieves us of uncertainty concerning the future, and of regrets over the past, while at the same time it brings us into present fellowship with the Father whose we are.

Fourth, the Spirit of adoption brings us into heirship. Now we have "the firstfruits of the Spirit" (Rom. 8:23), and can have the foretastes of our inheritance (Eph. 1:13, 14). The incalculable wealth of this inheritance is all at our disposal. We are "heirs of God, and joint-heirs with Christ," for "if children, then heirs" (Rom. 8:17). To be a joint-heir with Christ does not mean that we share one half and He the other, but it means that all He has is ours too. To be an heir of God means that all the best that a Father of grace, love, and omnipotence can give us is our possession. Child of God, while we suffer with Him now, we can lift up our heads, for we have "unsearchable riches."

In Conclusion

Adoption delivers us from bondage to legalism. We are free to do as we please because we please to do only God's will. It delivers us from bondage to fear, which means deliverance from torment (I John 4:18). It delivers us from bondage to sin, the sin that only God can cancel by the blood of His Son, and that only God can overcome by the Spirit of His Son within.

Adoption brings us into fellowship with the Father. All men are creatures of God, but not all men are sons of God. Man as a creature of God can have an intellectual apprehension of Him, but only the man who has received His Son can have fellowship with Him: "And truly our fellowship is with the Father, and with his Son Jesus Christ" (I John 1:3).

Adoption connects us with the inexhaustible supply from which to draw. Now our God has promised to supply all our needs "according to his riches in glory by Christ Jesus" (Phil. 4:19), and these riches are ours for all eternity.

Adoption stretches before us the immeasurable hope that reaches from eternity to eternity. We need His Spirit to even meagerly perceive it, and we need all eternity to appropriate it. Oh the "exceeding riches of his grace in his kindness toward us through Christ Jesus" (Eph. 2:7)!

CHAPTER SEVEN

SANCTIFICATION

Definition of Sanctification

Sanctification is that work of grace whereby the believer is separated from self and inward sinfulness and, by the infilling of the Holy Spirit, set apart unto holiness and service. It marks a crisis subsequent to conversion when one is brought to see his need and appropriates God's provision for it.

Sanctification literally means "to make holy"; consequently the Holy Spirit is the necessary Agent in sanctification, and Christ is the adequate provision: Christ Jesus "is made unto us . . . sanctification" (I Cor. 1:30). There is no sanctification morally in the Scriptural sense apart from contact and union with Him.

Terms for Sanctification

There are various terms for the work of sanctification in the believer's life. This often results in confusion, especially on the part of the young and uninstructed Christian. It should be kept in mind, however, that these terms are like weather vanes on separate houses. They all show which way the wind is blowing, and they all point in the same direction. As individuals we may use the terms that seem the clearest to us and that help us to understand the work of sanctification, but other individuals may use other terms that are equally desirable to them. It is well, though, to use terms that are found in the Bible, and to so coordinate them that their one meaning is understood.

Here are some of the terms used by various Christian groups and teachers, which express this work in the believer's life: sanctification, perfect love, a pure heart, holiness, the victorious life, life on the highest plane, the deeper life, and the like. Each of these emphasizes some phase of the same experience.

Since the Holy Spirit is the indispensable Instrument in the sanctification of the believer, here are some Scriptural terms used of the Holy Spirit in connection with this work:

(1) The *baptism* with the Holy Spirit. "He [Jesus] shall baptize you with the Holy Ghost, and with fire" (Matt. 3:11). "Upon whom thou shalt see the Spirit descending, and remaining on him, the same is he which baptizeth with the Holy Ghost" (John 1:33). "But ye shall be baptized with the Holy Ghost not many days hence" (Acts 1:5). "But ye shall be baptized with the Holy Ghost" (Acts 11:16).

(2) The *filling* with the Holy Spirit. "And they were all filled with the Holy Ghost, and began to speak with other tongues, as the Spirit gave them utterance" (Acts 2:4). "And when they had prayed

..., they were all filled with the Holy Ghost, and they spake the word of God with boldness" (Acts 4:31).

(3) *Receiving* the Holy Spirit. This term is used more frequently than the other two. "But this spake he of the Spirit, which they that believe on him should receive" (John 7:39). "He breathed on them, and saith unto them, Receive ye the Holy Ghost" (John 20:22). "Repent, and be baptized ..., and ye shall receive the gift of the Holy Ghost" (Acts 2:38). "Then laid they their hands on them, and they received the Holy Ghost" (Acts 8:17). "Have ye received the Holy Ghost since ye believed?" (Acts 19:2). "Received ye the Spirit by the works of the law, or by the hearing of faith?" (Gal. 3:2).

It will be noticed that in the Scriptures the Holy Spirit uses these three terms, *baptize, fill, receive,* interchangeably (e.g., John 7:39 and Acts 2:38; cf. Acts 1:5, Acts 2:4). It is well, therefore, to keep this in mind and not quibble over terms that have the divine sanction of Scriptural usage.

The Objects of Sanctification

In the first place, the infilling with the Holy Spirit, with His consequent sanctifying work, is not for the world. The unbeliever is in no condition to actively receive the Holy Spirit: "And I will pray the Father, and he shall give you another Comforter, .. whom the world cannot receive, because it seeth him not, neither knoweth him" (John 14:16, 17). What the unbeliever needs is the regenerating work of the Holy Spirit. Not till then is he in a position to understand spiritually anything about the Holy Spirit.

In the second place, sanctification is for the Church. It is Christ's bride who is the recipient of this work of the Spirit: "... Christ also loved the church, and gave himself for it; that he might sanctify and cleanse it with the washing of water by the word" (Eph. 5:25b, 26). It is quite appropriate and necessary that the bride of the Lamb should be holy: "His wife hath made herself ready" (Rev. 19:7).

In the third place, sanctification is for each individual member of the Church, Christ's body. A sick member can affect the whole body. A body has no more health than each of its members. Christ prayed that as individuals His disciples might be sanctified: "Sanctify them through thy truth" (John 17:17). Paul prayed that each believer might in every part of his being—spirit, soul, and body—be sanctified: "And the very God of peace sanctify you wholly; and I pray God your whole spirit and soul and body be preserved blameless unto the coming of our Lord Jesus Christ" (I Thess. 5:23). On the day of Pentecost Peter declared that each individual who repented and turned to Christ would receive the Holy Spirit: "Repent, and be baptized *every one of you* ..., and ye shall receive the gift of the Holy Ghost" (Acts 2:38). The Holy Spirit who was outpoured on that day was distributed to individuals as cloven tongues of fire "on *each* of them" (Acts 2:3). Sanctification is not received *en masse* but individually and personally. This places upon each of us the opportunity of responding and the privilege of receiving.

The Purpose of Sanctification

Sanctification is for the purpose of *meeting man's inmost need*. That need is graphically set forth in Romans 7. There is an inner foe called "the law of sin" (v. 23). It takes the regenerating work of the Spirit to cause one to "delight in the law of God" (v. 22). It takes a revelation by the same Spirit to show him that "in me . . . dwelleth no good thing" (v. 18).

When we come to Christ for salvation, we are concerned with the sins we have committed against Him. To be born again means the canceling of those sins and the blessing of fellowship with God. But the "law of sin" that causes us to commit sins is usually not discovered until later, as the Holy Spirit leads us on in the light. Then it is that we cry out for deliverance not from the guilt of sins we have committed but from the bondage of our sinful nature which causes us to commit them. Is there no remedy for this inmost need? Thank God there is.

The Holy Spirit takes us right back to the cross, and there we see that Christ not only died for our sins but also for our sinfulness. "God sending his own Son in the likeness of sinful flesh, and for sin, condemned sin in the flesh" (Rom. 8:3). The death sentence has been passed upon this inner law of sin, and a new law, "the law of the Spirit of life in Christ Jesus" (Rom. 8:2), takes its place. Christ not only died for our *sins*, but God "hath made him to be *sin* for us" (II. Cor. 5:21).

This is God's *provision*. But how may we experience the *appropriation* of it? By *identification* with Christ in His death. We must consent to die with Christ in His death. We must climb upon the cross with Him, and with our whole will yield over the self that has caused all our trouble. *Crucifixion* is the only way of deliverance: "I am crucified with Christ" (Gal. 2:20).

What does all this have to do with sanctification? Simply this—the Holy Spirit will not sanctify the self life, or the sinful nature. This has to be identified with Christ on the cross before the Holy Spirit can perform His sanctifying, infilling work. It may be true that our understanding of all this may be vague at the time we yield to the Spirit's infilling, but He will faithfully lead us on, and whatever light He gives us in the future is undimmed by the fact that all controversy was settled when we yielded ourselves to Him.

The purpose of sanctification, then, is to give us deliverance from self and sin and to show us God's way of victory: "Walk in the Spirit, and ye shall not fulfill the lust of the flesh" (Gal. 5:16).

There is another purpose in sanctification and the infilling of the Spirit, and that is *to empower us for service*. Though Jesus knew the harvest was great and the need was crying in His ears, yet He commanded His disciples, "Tarry ye in the city of Jerusalem, until ye be endued with power from on high" (Luke 24:49). Before He ascended, He promised, "But ye shall receive power, after that the Holy Ghost is come upon you: and ye shall be witnesses unto me ..." (Acts 1:8). Because the disciples tarried until the Holy Spirit was outpoured upon them, they did more for the Lord in one day than they could have done in many months of service without the Spirit's power. God's recipe is the same today. Without an individual enduement of the Spirit, no person is prepared to be an effective witness. When will God's people learn not only *God's program*—"Go ye therefore, and teach all nations"—but also *God's method*—"endued with power from on high"? The sooner we comply with God's method, the sooner will His program be fulfilled.

The purpose, then, of the sanctifying, infilling work of the Holy Spirit is twofold—for victory in Christian living, and for power in service for Him.

The Aspects of Sanctification

Sanctification has both *ritualistic and moral aspects*. The place where Moses stood at the burning bush was holy ritualistically because God was there. In the same way, the articles of furniture in the tabernacle, the tabernacle itself, and in later days the temple were holy. Also certain days were holy because they had been set apart for special ceremonial observances.

Moral sanctification is applicable to persons only. Jesus, however, did not need moral sanctification, for He "knew no sin" (II Cor. 5:21). He came to do

God's will, and delighted therein (Heb. 10:7; Psa. 40: 6–8). The only sense in which He could sanctify himself (John 17:19) was, therefore, in this ceremonial aspect of His dedication to the work for which He had come. In the case of believers, however, they need moral sanctification because of the innate sinfulness of the human heart.

Sanctification also has both *negative and positive aspects*. Negatively it is separation *from*, thus setting the recipient apart. This is intimately related to the positive side of sanctification, which is dedication *unto*. The purpose of separation *from* is that dedication *unto* might take place. In the sanctification of persons this separation is from sin and self, and the dedication is unto God. This dedication to God brings us into contact with Him and imparts to us His holiness. It is by this contact only that we are sanctified in the sense of being made holy. The only way in which we can sanctify ourselves is in this negative aspect of separation. The positive aspect of being made holy is God's work alone and comes through our being in touch with the Holy One.

Sanctification has both *objective and subjective aspects*. Failure to see this distinction often confuses one in his understanding of the work. Objectively, all this work is in Christ. It is one finished work. Christ is made unto us sanctification (I Cor. 1:30). But subjectively, this finished work is made real to us only by our personal appropriation. Objectively, we see what Christ did *for* us: we "have been sanctified through the offering of the body of Jesus Christ once for all" (Heb. 10:10, A.R.V.). But subjectively, this must become experiential *in* us as we see our need and yield to Him.

Means of Sanctification

In the work of sanctification there are both the human and divine sides. On the divine side the work is complete.

(1) We are sanctified by the Word of God. Jesus prayed, "Sanctify them through thy truth: thy word is truth" (John 17:17). The Word has a cleansing effect; it washes (Eph. 5:26). The Word also has a penetrating effect; it pierces (Heb. 4:12).

(2) We are sanctified by the blood of Jesus: "Wherefore Jesus also, that he might sanctify the people *with his own blood*, suffered without the gate" (Heb. 13:12). The blood of Jesus is the basis for all our purity and victory. Whenever the Holy Spirit deals with us for either our sinful acts or our sinful nature, He always takes us back to the cross.

(3) Our sanctification is a work of the Trinity. We are sanctified by *God the Father*: "And the very God of peace sanctify you wholly" (I Thess. 5:23). We are sanctified by *Jesus Christ*: "For both he [cf. context, referring to Jesus] that sanctifieth and they who are sanctified are all of one" (Heb. 2:11); Christ had our sanctification in mind when He suffered and died for us. We are sanctified by the *Holy Spirit*: "God hath from the beginning chosen you to salvation through sanctification of the Spirit and belief of the truth" (II Thess. 2:13) "Elect ... through sanctification of the Spirit" (I Pet. 1:2). Since the Triune God is working toward our sanctification, we are wise indeed to cooperate.

On the human side *separation* is the first step. Whether we are to be a vessel unto honor depends upon this: "If a man therefore purge himself from these, he shall be a vessel unto honor, sanctified, and meet for the Master's use, and prepared unto every good work" (II Tim. 2:21). The reason God doesn't use some persons is that they have never set themselves apart so He could.

Then comes the step of *dedication*. Dedication is something we do; it involves our will, and it includes our whole being. "I beseech you therefore brethren ... that ye present your bodies a living sacrifice, holy acceptable unto God, which is your reasonable service" (Rom. 12:1). Note that in this verse, dedication is an act for Christians—"brethren." Note, too, that it is not giving up sinful habits, but it is offering to God an acceptable sacrifice that is both "living" and "holy." This is a voluntary act. God does not coerce us, but beseeches us to do so on the basis of His mercies. It is a complete act. Obviously if God has our bodies, He also has our whole being—spirit and soul as well. It is an inclusive and specific act: "But yield yourselves unto God, as those that are alive from the dead, and your members as instruments of righteousness unto God" (Rom. 6:13). "Even so now yield your members servants of righteousness unto holiness" (Rom. 6:19). To yield to God our members means to give Him our mental and spiritual faculties together with our whole body, hands, feet, eyes, ears, tongue. This is the offering God seeks more than any other, and there is no victorious living or power in service without it.

The step of *faith* is the final one. When our dedication to God is unquestionable, faith is unhindered. The man who dares commit himself to God, by that very act dares to trust Him. When Peter was recounting God's work in the home of Cornelius, he declared God purified "their hearts by faith" (Acts 15:9). When Paul was relating his own conversion, he told how God had commissioned him to go to the Gentiles "that they may receive forgiveness of sins, and inheritance among them which are sanctified by faith that is in me" (Acts 26:18). When our faith is placed in God, it has both the right objective and the right basis.

Illustrations of Sanctification

There are many illustrations and types of sanctification. A few are cited. The court of the tabernacle in the wilderness had two articles of furniture: first, there was the brazen altar, where judgment for sin took place, and animals were sacrificed; second, there was the laver of water, where cleansing was provided. "Let us draw near . . . , having our hearts sprinkled from an evil conscience, and our bodies washed with pure water" (Heb. 10:22).

The cleansing of the leper is illustrative. When the leper was pronounced clean, he went through ritualistic performances, among which was the offering of the trespass offering and the anointing with oil. The blood of the trespass offering was placed upon his right ear (for right hearing), his right thumb (for right service), and the great toe of his right foot (for right walking). Then the priest placed on top of the blood the anointing oil, on ear, hand, and foot (Lev. 14:12–18). The cleansing with blood is the prerequisite for the outpouring of oil, typifying the Holy Spirit.

One of the clearest types is the crossing of the Jordan. Hebrews chapter 3:17 through chapter 4: 11 makes certain that crossing the Jordan is an experience for Christians in this life, and that there is a land of Canaan which is better than the wilderness life. "Let us labor therefore to enter into that rest, lest any man fall after the same example of unbelief" (Heb. 4:11).

Among *historic examples* in the Old Testament, Jacob is one of the most impressive. After he met God at Bethel, meaning "the house of God" (Gen. 28:10–22), he encountered much trouble and conflict; but most of it came because of his own tricky nature. When he later met God at Peniel, meaning "the face of God" (Gen. 32:22–32), and confessed that his name was Jacob (whereby he confessed his evil nature)—the magnetic center of his whole life was transferred from his own interests to God's.

The historic examples in the Book of Acts are enlightening. It was *on believers* that the Holy Spirit was outpoured in Acts 2. When Peter preached to the people, he did not tell them that since the Holy Spirit had thus been outpoured dispensationally, such outpouring settled the matter for them individually. He told them to repent and be baptized in the name of Jesus Christ "unto the remission of your sins; and ye shall receive the gift of the Holy Spirit" (Acts 2:38, A.R.V.). It was *for believers* that Peter and John prayed in order that these converts in Philip's Samaritan revival might receive the Holy Spirit (Acts 8:14–17). When Paul met certain converts of John the Baptist in Ephesus, he asked them the all-important question, "Have ye received the Holy Ghost since ye believed?" It makes no particular difference whether one translates this question "since" or "when" ye believed. The very fact that Paul asked the question certifies that one may believe without receiving the Holy Spirit, for receiving implies something active on the believer's part. Since these converts knew only John's baptism, they were therefore baptized in the name of Jesus. But note, Paul did not let them go till he had prayed that they might receive the Holy Spirit (Acts 19:1–7). Would that all preachers had this same concern for their converts.

Results of Sanctification

Briefly and in summary, some of the results of sanctification are these: (1) Enduement (Acts 1:8). Power for witnessing comes through Christ's Agent, the Holy Spirit. (2) Victory over sin: "Walk in the Spirit, and ye shall not fulfill the lust of the flesh" (Gal. 5:16). "But if by the Spirit ye put to death the deeds of the body, ye shall live" (Rom. 8:13). "Likewise reckon ye also yourselves to be dead indeed unto sin, but alive unto God through Jesus Christ our Lord" (Rom. 6:11). (3) Fruitfulness is another result. All the Christian qualities that one can desire are produced by the Spirit (Gal. 5:22, 23). If we want to be a blessing, we must be filled with the Holy Spirit.

This guarantees "the fulness of the blessing of the gospel of Christ" to others (Rom. 15:29).

Maintaining Sanctification

In order to maintain any new step we have taken with the Lord, *obedience* is a prime requisite. God gives the Holy Spirit "to them that obey him" (Acts 5: 32). It is possible to grieve the Holy Spirit (Eph. 4:30), or to quench Him (I Thess. 5:19). We must guard against these conditions. But whenever there has been failure, we must at once confess it to God and receive His forgiveness (I John 1:9).

In the final analysis, sanctification is not an abstract quality but a Person—Christ Jesus, who is made unto us sanctification (I Cor. 1:30). *Abiding* in Christ is an essential requisite. We must give time to Him by reading His Word and by daily prayer. Abiding is the secret of power: "He that abideth in me, and I in him, the same bringeth forth much fruit: for without me ye can do nothing" (John 15:5). Abiding is also the secret of victory: "Whosoever abideth in him sinneth not" (I John 3:6). When Christ has all *of* us, He is all *to* us.

Progress in Sanctification

One of the best things about our life in the Lord Jesus Christ is that we keep developing. There is definitely a progressive side to sanctification, and this must not be overlooked. To feel we have arrived only betrays how little progress we have made and how far we yet have to go. The Holy Spirit keeps giving us light, and as we walk in it, the blood keeps cleans-

ıg us (I John 1:7). "For by one offering hath he per-
ᵉcted for evermore them who are being made holy"
Heb. 10:14, Rotherham). We are told to cleanse our-
ᵉlves "from all filthiness of the flesh and spirit, per-
ᵉcting holiness in the fear of God" (II Cor. 7:1). One
f the last exhortations in view of the Lord's coming
, "He that is holy, let him be made holy yet more"
Rev. 22:11, A.R.V. m.).

The vows taken at the marriage altar are just the
ᵉginning of a new life entailing many adjustments
ιd victories. After crossing Jordan there are many
ᵒnquests in the land of Canaan. The crisis is only an
ιtroduction into a new realm. "Therefore leaving the
ᵣinciples of the doctrine of Christ, let us go on unto
ᵉrfection" (Heb. 6:1).

CHAPTER EIGHT

PRAYER

Definition of Prayer

Prayer is communication, through the merits of the blood of Jesus Christ and on the basis of His atoning work, between man and the personal, eternal, infinite God and Father of our Lord Jesus Christ.

Prayer is not thinking good thoughts. It is all right to think good thoughts, but this is not praying. "Which of you by taking thought can add one cubit unto his stature?" (Matt. 6:27). To pray in the Scriptural sense is to communicate with another Person, and that Other is God.

Prayer is not self-meditation. Self-meditation simply takes us around in circles, but prayer contacts us with the throne of God: "After this manner therefore pray ye: Our Father which art in heaven" (Matt. 6:9).

Prayer is not an appeal to any earthly person or heavenly saint, but a direct approach to God through the one Mediator, Christ Jesus: "For there is one God, and one mediator between God and men, the man Christ Jesus" (I Tim. 2:5).

To Whom Do We Pray

The whole Trinity is involved in our praying. When we pray to the Triune God, we are not praying to three gods but to the one eternal and infinite Being. However, since there are personal distinctions in the Trinity, prayer is often addressed to God the Father: "For through him [Jesus Christ] we both [Jew and Gentile, cf. context] have access by one Spirit unto the Father" (Eph. 2:18). "For this cause I bow my knees unto the Father of our Lord Jesus Christ" (Eph. 3:14).

Prayer is also addressed to Jesus, the Son. The martyr Stephen prayed, "Lord Jesus, receive my spirit" (Acts 7:59). Paul refers to "all that in every place call upon the name of Jesus Christ our Lord" (I Cor. 1:2).

In one instance, at least, prayer is addressed to the Spirit, but this is at God's command: "Then said he unto me, Prophesy unto the wind [breath, or Spirit] . . . , Come from the four winds, O breath, and breathe upon these slain, that they may live" (Ezek. 37:9). It is quite customary, however, to pray to the Spirit in some of our hymns and choruses.

It seems the usual procedure is to pray to the Father in the name of Jesus Christ by the inditement of the Holy Spirit. One should not be conscious, however, of the form in which he is praying, for the essence of prayer is communication with God, and the Holy Spirit cuts His own channel through the praying heart.

But it should always be borne in mind that prayer is to a *personal* Being, and that prayer is not a matter of self-help and improvement through a mental gymnastic. Prayer reaches out objectively to One who, through Jesus Christ our Lord, is known as our Father and who answers the prayer prayed in Jesus' name.

The Basis of Prayer

All religions have some form of prayer, but only Christianity has the proper basis. That basis is the redemptive work of Jesus Christ. God hears the prayer of the penitent—"God be merciful to me a sinner" (Luke 18:13)—and can forgive because Christ died to procure that forgiveness.

God also hears the prayers of His children because they come to Him through the merits of Jesus Christ. "And whatsoever ye shall ask in my name, that will I do, that the Father may be glorified in the Son. If ye shall ask any thing in my name, I will do it" (John 14:13, 14).

It is because of and by means of Christ's redemptive work that we are told to draw near to God. "Having therefore, brethren, boldness to enter into the holiest by the blood of Jesus, by a new and living way which he hath consecrated for us . . . , let us draw near . . ." (Heb. 10:19–22). Among the many benefits that the death of Christ has purchased for us, access to God through prayer is one of the most blessed.

Phases of Prayer

There are various words for prayer in the New Testament, each one representing some phase.

One word means *to pray, to beseech*. It is used in Matt. 9:38, where Jesus tells us to "*pray* ye therefore the Lord of the harvest that he will send forth laborers into his harvest." And again in Luke 21:36: "Watch ye therefore, and *pray* always that ye may be accounted worthy to escape all these things that shall come to pass . . . ." It is also used when Jesus told Peter that He had prayed for him that his faith would not fail (Luke 22:32), and elsewhere.

Another word means *to ask* in the sense of *to request*. There are thirteen places where this word is used, the first instance being in Luke 4:38, where "they *besought*" Jesus for the healing of Simon's wife's mother.

It is interesting to note that this word is used by Jesus in John 14:16—"I will pray the Father"—in connection with the coming of the Comforter. It is also used in His prayer for the disciples in John 17:9—"I pray for them" (also vv. 15, 20).

There is a word that means *to pray, to wish*. "Now I *pray* to God that ye do no evil" (II Cor. 13:7). "Pray one for another" (James 5:16).

Another interesting word means *to call, to summon alongside of*. Jesus said that He could pray the Father for twelve legions of angels (Matt. 26:53), thus summoning them alongside of Him. Paul in vision saw a man of Macedonia who "prayed him" to come over and help them (Acts 16:9), again summoning him to come alongside of them.

The most common word for prayer means *to offer prayers to God*. It is used about eighty-one times. Jesus instructed, "After this manner pray ye" (Matt. 6:9). We are to "watch and pray" (Matt. 26:41), and to "pray without ceasing" (I Thess. 5:17).

Another word means *supplication*. It refers to prayers imploring God's aid in some particular matter. Paul expected deliverance through the *prayers* of the Philippians (Phil. 1:19). He also valued the prayers of the Corinthians: "Ye also helping together by prayer for us" (II Cor. 1:11). God's ears are open to our prayers (I Pet. 3:12), and the effectual, fervent prayer of a righteous man avails much (James 5:16).

There is another word that has the idea of an *unrestricted pouring out* to God. It is connected with fasting in Matthew 17:21. An angel adds incense to the prayers of the saints in Revelation 8:4. Paul uses this word fourteen times in his epistles.

The highest form of prayer is *intercession*, literally meaning "a falling in with, an interview, a coming together." Paul asks that "intercessions . . . be made for all men" (I Tim. 2:1). In this kind of praying we do not come for ourselves, but we take the place of another. It is converse with God in childlike confidence.

The above list is more than an array of words. It is a revelation of our approach to God. Our Father has encouraged us to come. Thus, with these various phases of praying spread before us, with the way available through Jesus Christ, and with God's ear opened, there is no excuse for not praying.

Why We Should Pray

We should pray because it is *God's command*. Jesus said, "Men ought always to pray, and not to faint" (Luke 18:1). This should settle the question. "Be careful for nothing; but in every thing by prayer and supplication ... let your requests be made known unto God" (Phil. 4:6). If we would obey this command more, we would have less care. "Pray without ceasing" (I Thess. 5:17) is as much a command as any other. The avenue of prayer should always be kept open.

We should pray because we have been *taught to do so* by Jesus himself. On one occasion the disciples were listening to Jesus pray. They respectfully listened until He was through, and then requested, "Lord, teach us to pray." In answer to their request Jesus gave them the pattern prayer, "Our Father which art in heaven ..." (Luke 11:1, 2). Instead of giving them a preparatory course in prayer, He launched them right into the business of praying by telling them to address God directly. The way to learn to pray is to start praying. Prayer is the normal cry of the child to the Father in the heart of him who has been born again by God's Spirit through faith in Jesus Christ.

The *promises of God* should also cause us to pray. Verily "He is a rewarder of them that diligently seek him" (Heb. 11:6). "Ask, and it shall be given you; seek, and ye shall find; knock, and it shall be opened unto you: For every one that asketh receiveth; and he that seeketh findeth; and to him that knocketh it shall be opened" (Matt. 7:7, 8). It may well be that our failure to have prayer answered is that we have not prayed: "Ye have not because ye ask not" (James 4:2). There are many promises connected with prayer. Such a foundation can never fail. To stand on God's promise, and to pray in faith is to receive His answer. The answer may be "no," or it may be "yes"; but we shall hear from heaven, and that is sufficient.

Examples of praying men and their prayers in the Bible are enough to cause us to pray. Jesus' own example should never be overlooked; He got alone to pray to the Father. Prayer was vital to His program. Abraham prayed; his intercession for Sodom (Gen. 18:23–33) is classic. Moses prayed; his place as a mediator demanded his praying even to the extent of offering his life in his intercession for the sinning Israelites (Ex. 32:31, 32). The story of Nehemiah is inaugurated with his prayer (Neh. 1:4–11), and the record of his accomplishment is shot through with prayer. The prophets prayed, the apostles prayed, the early church prayed. Who will pray today? Let no one say it is too costly to pray. It is too costly not to pray.

Prayer is a *spiritual law*. God has chosen this method. It is the appropriate method to use in dealing with self-determining, personal beings. He could have used some other method, but He has not chosen to do so. For some inscrutable reason He has willed to take man into partnership with Him in prayer. From our point of view it seems that God has limited himself to our praying. This should incite us to awe and reverential response. To neglect prayer is to neglect the highest function of the Christian life and the most profound opportunity for ministry ever offered to human beings.

Who May Pray

The one who is not willing to give up sin cannot expect to pray with confidence that God hears him. "If I regard iniquity in my heart, the LORD will not hear me" (Psa. 66:18). This does not mean that penitent sinners cannot pray, but that those who are impenitent and rebellious can expect no answer from God. If we want God to meet us, we must meet God's terms.

Any one, no matter how great a sinner, can pray if he prays in penitence. The publican prayed, "God be merciful to me *the* sinner" (Luke 18:13, A.R.V. m.). He, like Paul, felt himself the chief of sinners. God heard his prayer, and answered him. God always hears such a cry. Let every sinner take heart.

God hears the prayer of the righteous: "The eyes of the LORD are upon the righteous, and his ears are open unto their cry" (Psa. 34:15). And again, "He heareth the prayer of the righteous" (Prov. 15:29). In fact, "the prayer of the righteous is his delight" (Prov. 15:8). We are encouraged to approach God in prayer: "For this shall every one that is godly pray unto thee in a time when thou mayest be found" (Psa. 32:6). The godly man has God's ear.

Obedience produces confidence in prayer: "And whatsoever we ask, we receive of him because we keep his commandments, and do those things that are pleasing in his sight" (I John 3:22). A yielded heart is a prayerful heart.

In summary, those who abide in Christ are always on praying ground: "If ye abide in me, and my words abide in you, ye shall ask what ye will, and it shall be done unto you" (John 15:7). Prayer keeps us abiding, and abiding encourages prayer.

How to Pray

First, *negatively*, there are instructions how not to pray. Jesus told us not to use *vain repetition*. Such praying is only much speaking without reaching the ear of God. "But when ye pray, use not vain repetition as the heathen do: for they think that they shall be heard for their much speaking" (Matt. 6:7). When we pray to God, we do not need to repeat phrases, or even repetitiously speak His name. Our praying should be as orderly and direct as any conversation we carry on with an earthly friend.

We should not pray *to be seen and heard of men*. "And when thou prayest, thou shalt not be as the hypocrites are: for they love to pray standing in the synagogues and in the corners of the streets, that they may be seen of men" (Matt. 6:5). It is possible to pray in church because we want someone present to hear what we think of them and their foolish practices. Or it is possible to pray because we want the audience to see how charmingly we can talk to God. This kind of praying carries its own reward, but not one that comes from heaven.

We should not pray *in unbelief*. "But let him ask in faith, nothing wavering. For he that wavereth is like a wave of the sea, driven with the wind and tossed.

114

For let not that man think that he shall receive any
thing of the Lord" (James 1:6, 7). This does not mean
we cannot pray if we have doubts and if our faith is
weak. Our very praying, if we tell God our condition,
will help us to believe Him. But it does mean that unless we have faith that God will hear us, our coming
to Him is in vain. If we come merely as an experiment
or just to please someone else, and not because we have
a personal desire to do so, we have no confidence in
the God to whom we appeal. We do not have to remain
out in the storm with the winds lashing us back and
forth, driven and tossed. Our very need should drive
us to prayer and into the haven of rest.

We should not pray *amiss*. To pray amiss is to
pray with a selfish motive; it is to ask God for un-
warranted things merely for our own enjoyment. "Ye
ask, and receive not because ye ask amiss, that ye
may consume it upon your lusts" (James 4:3). This
does not mean that God does not delight in giving
good things to His children. "Every good gift and every
perfect gift . . . cometh down from the Father of lights"
(James 1:17). But our desires need to be purged for
our own good. A box of chocolates in the hands of
a young child is a liability. God knows how harmful
some of the things He has withheld would have been
to us.

On the *positive side*, we should pray *in the name
of Jesus Christ*. "Whatsoever ye shall ask the Father
in my name, he will give it you" (John 16:23). This
means more than merely appending the phrase, "in
Jesus' name," to our petitions. It means to pray that

kind of prayer that the Son of God can endorse. A forged check will not pass at the bank of heaven. That is why abiding in Jesus Christ is a requirement for receiving what we ask: "If ye abide in me, and my words abide in you, ye shall ask what ye will, and it shall be done unto you" (John 15:7). We are so one with the Lord that our will is lost in His, and what we will is His will. The prayer that works is not only the kind that puts its amen to God's promises, but the kind to which Jesus can also put His amen.

We should pray *through the agency of the Holy Spirit*: "Likewise the Spirit also helpeth our infirmities: for we know not what we should pray for as we ought: but the Spirit itself maketh intercession for us with groanings which cannot be uttered" (Rom. 8:26). True praying comes from the throne of God and is sent back to the throne of God as the Spirit finds yielded, believing hearts as His channels. The Spirit-taught believer is the praying believer.

We should pray *earnestly*. Elijah is an example: "Elias ... prayed earnestly that it might not rain" (James 5:17). Literally, he prayed "with prayer" (A.R.V. m.). Prayer to him was no farce. Merely to go through the performance of praying is not praying. Praying should be "with prayer." Perfunctory praying is weak praying or no praying at all. To pray earnestly does not mean to pray emotionally. The prophets of Baal did that, but there was no fire. Earnest praying takes effort, the choice of the will and the channeling of the emotions. If we always waited till we felt like praying, we should miss a lot of it. Earnest praying is the kind that gets at it, and prays.

Fasting and prayer often go together. Moses (Deut. 9:9), Ezra (Ezra 8:21), Daniel (Dan. 9:3; 10:2, 3), and other Old Testament saints fasted. The Master fasted. The early church fasted (Acts 13:2, 3; 14:23). Why should not we fast? There is no merit in fasting itself, but there is merit in relieving ourselves of physical demands to build up the inner man and to partake of the meat that others know not of (John 4:32).

Thanksgiving and prayer also go together: "In every thing by prayer and supplication with thanksgiving let your requests be made known unto God" (Phil. 4:6). "Continue in prayer, and watch in the same with thanksgiving" (Col. 4:2). If we would put more thanksgiving into our praying, we should enjoy our praying more. Thanksgiving is the salt that adds flavor to the banquet of worship. Thanksgiving is the fragrance that comes from the incense of prayer.

We should pray *in union with others*: "If two of you shall agree on earth as touching any thing that they shall ask, it shall be done for them of my Father which is in heaven" (Matt. 18:19). To agree means to *symphonize*, to sound together, to harmonize. Jangling discord is not prayer. There is a place for agreed praying with others. This unison of prayer brings back the answer like an echo from the harmony of believers in accord.

There is also a place for *private praying* in our closet alone with our Father "in secret" (Matt. 6:6). No other kind of praying takes the place of this. Praying in accord with others is made by those who have met God alone for themselves. If one depends on group praying and fails to meet God for himself, he will soon find his spiritual life drained. Our source of supply is from God.

It goes without saying that we should pray *believingly*. "Lord, teach us to pray" should sometimes be changed to "Lord, give us Thy faith." Faith claims the answer. "And all things, whatsoever ye shall ask in prayer, believing, ye shall receive" (Matt. 21:22). Unbelief probably accounts for more unanswered prayer than any other one thing.

We should pray *unceasingly*: "Pray without ceasing" (I Thess. 5:17). How can one stay on his knees all the time? Since prayer is the language of the heart, the heart that is right with God will be a perpetual channel of prayer whether or not one is on his knees. The heart that is true to its lover unceasingly loves. And so it is with prayer. One might as well ask, "How can I breathe all the time?" As long as there is physical life, there must be breath. And spiritual life demands breathing too, and that breathing is prayer. Necessarily duties and legitimate occupations may draw one's attention, but this does not draw the heart away from the prayer connection. To love God with all the heart is to have a praying heart.

CHAPTER NINE

TOPICS FOR DISCUSSION

REPENTANCE

. How would you explain repentance to a self-righteous person?

. How would you explain true repentance to a person who is sorry only because he's been caught in his sin?

. What would you say to someone who is seemingly sorry for his sin but has never broken from it?

. What should be your reaction towards someone who comes to restore something he has stolen?

. Why should repentance be preached nowadays?

. What kind of preaching is most effective for producing repentance?

Why should believers repent? And from what?

What kind of living encourages others to repent?

What is the relationship of repentance to faith? to forgiveness? to conversion?

Is repentance an end in itself or a means to an end?

What is to be achieved through repentance?

Note several examples of repentance in the Bible.

Compare them with several examples of repentance from your own observation and experience.

FAITH

1. What are the characteristics of faith?
2. Describe the difference between faith and hope.
3. What is the relation of faith to works?
4. What is the relation of faith to assurance?
5. How does faith relate to other experiences of the Christian life?
6. What is the basis of faith?
7. Describe the stages of faith and how to advance therein.
8. What is the origin of faith?
9. How does a person maintain faith?
10. What is the importance of faith to Christian living?
11. How does faith become a reality instead of just theory?
12. List several exploits of faith from the past.
13. Describe an exploit of faith from the present.

CONVERSION

1. What is the difference between Christian conversion and other types of conversion?
2. What are the characteristics of one who is merely converted to some Christian leader or creed?
3. What are the characteristics of one who is truly converted to Christ.
4. What is the relationship of conversion to repentance? to faith? to Christian growth?
5. What does God expect from a convert to Christ?
6. What do men expect from a convert to Christ?
7. How should we live and preach so as to persuade others to follow Christ?

8. What is God's responsibility in the work of conversion?
9. What is man's responsibility in the work of conversion?
10. What should be the outcome of conversion?

REGENERATION

1. Is man totally depraved? And if so, what was the cause and the remaining evidences of this state?
2. Contrast reformation with regeneration.
3. What is the relationship of regeneration to righteous living?
4. Why do we have church membership, and for whom?
5. What is the place of baptism in the believer's life?
6. Why is childlikeness required of those who believe in Christ?
7. How is believing related to regeneration?
8. What is the relationship of God's Word to regeneration?
9. Define the work of the Holy Spirit in regeneration.
10. What is God's purpose in regenerating us and how do we experience the fulfillment of this goal?

JUSTIFICATION

1. For whom is justification?
2. Why can't we be justified by the law?
3. Contrast justification with forgiveness.
4. Compare and contrast justification and regeneration.
5. Why is God alone the only source of justification?
6. How can God justify the sinner without impeaching

His character?

7. How can justification be personally appropriated?
8. Compare and contrast the extent of justification with the extent of the atonement.
9. What are the benefits of justification?
10. What does God expect of me as a justified person?

ADOPTION

1. How is adoption related to regeneration and justification?
2. Name and explain the three tenses of adoption.
3. What does it mean to believe in and receive Jesus Christ?
4. How is adoption related to the law?
5. How is adoption related to deliverance from fear?
6. What effect does adoption have on our present righteous living?
7. How is adoption related to assurance?
8. Show how our inheritance is dependent upon adoption.
9. How is fellowship with God related to adoption?
10. When and what is the culmination of adoption?

SANCTIFICATION

1. Contrast God's part and man's part in the work of sanctification.
2. What is the nature and purpose of dedication to God?
3. What does the crisis step in sanctification do for us?
4. What does the process of sanctification do for us?
5. How do we maintain victorious Christian living?
6. Cite several illustrations, types, and examples of sanctification in the Bible.

7. What terms for sanctification appeal most to you and why?
8. Why do Christians need the infilling of the Holy Spirit?
9. What is the means of becoming Spirit-filled?
.0. What are the evidences of being Spirit-filled?
.1. What is the work of the cross in relation to victory over sinfulness?
2. What is the work of the cross in relation to the Spirit's infilling?
3. Show how Christ is our sanctification and our Sanctifier.

PRAYER

1. What is the difference between Christian praying and the prayers of other religions?
2. Why is a personal knowledge of God necessary in order to pray to Him?
3. How is Christ's work on the cross related to prayer?
4. List several scriptural encouragements and commands to pray.
5. Relate some of the effects of prayer in your own life and in the lives of others you know.
6. What are some practical prayer helps you have learned by experience?
7. What persons (both in the Bible and elsewhere) have stimulated you to pray, and how?
8. What are your greatest problems in prayer?
  How can Christians encourage more prayer among themselves?
  What should be our general objectives in prayer?
  How can we get answers to prayer?
  What is the importance of thanksgiving with prayer?